PILGRIMAGE

LOOKING AT GROUND ZERO

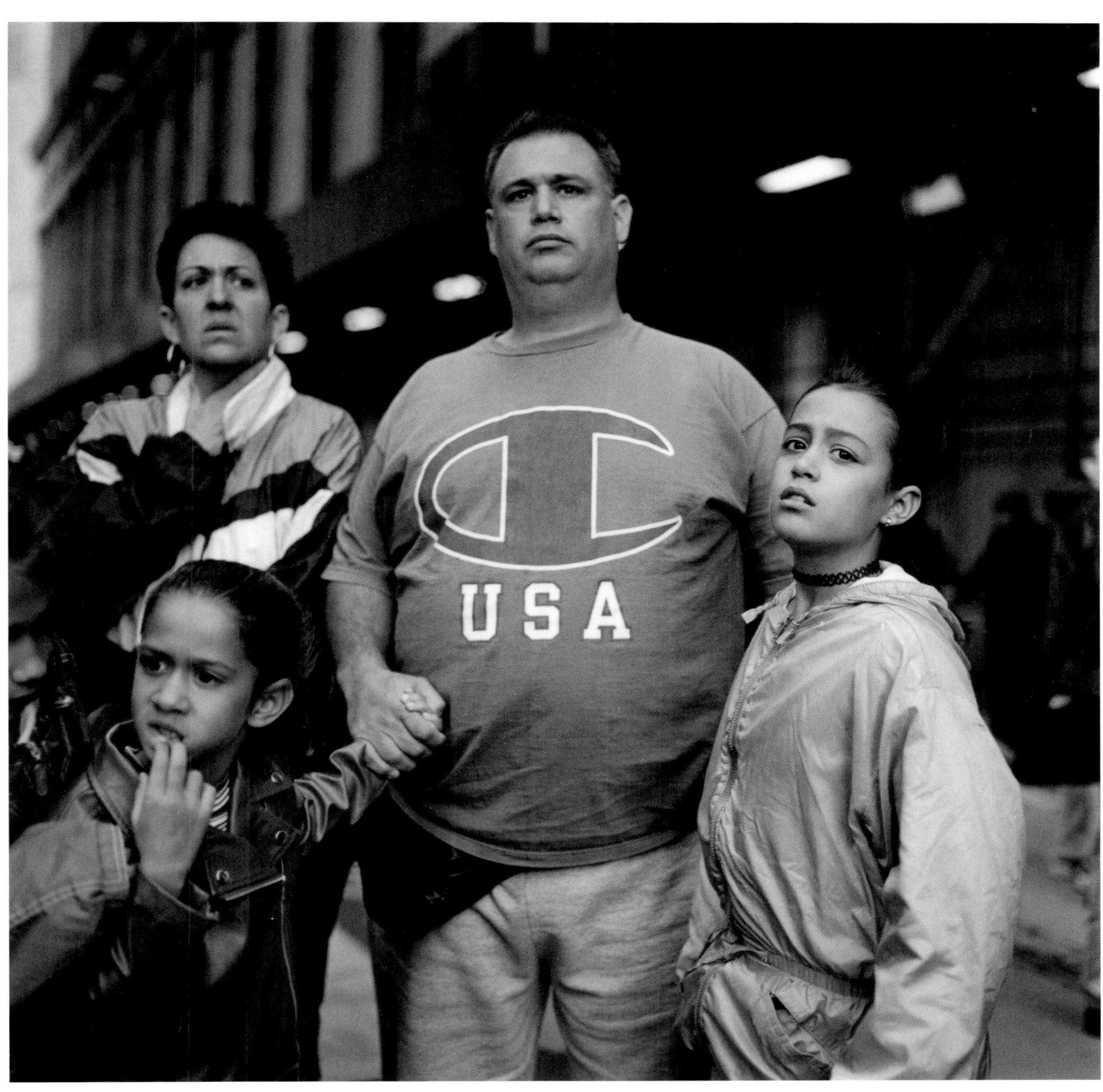
USA

PILGRIMAGE

LOOKING AT GROUND ZERO

Photographs by Kevin Bubriski

Afterword by Richard B. Woodward

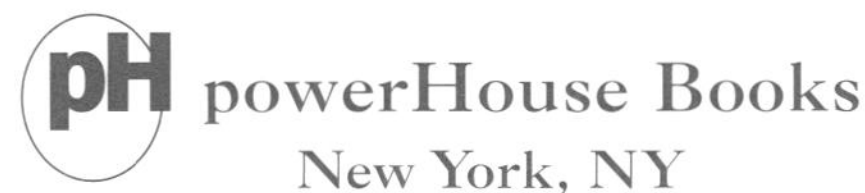

powerHouse Books
New York, NY

This book is dedicated to the victims of the attacks of September 11, and to their families and friends. This book is also dedicated to the individuals who appear in the photographs here, to all the others who have made the journey to Ground Zero, and to those who live and work in Lower Manhattan.

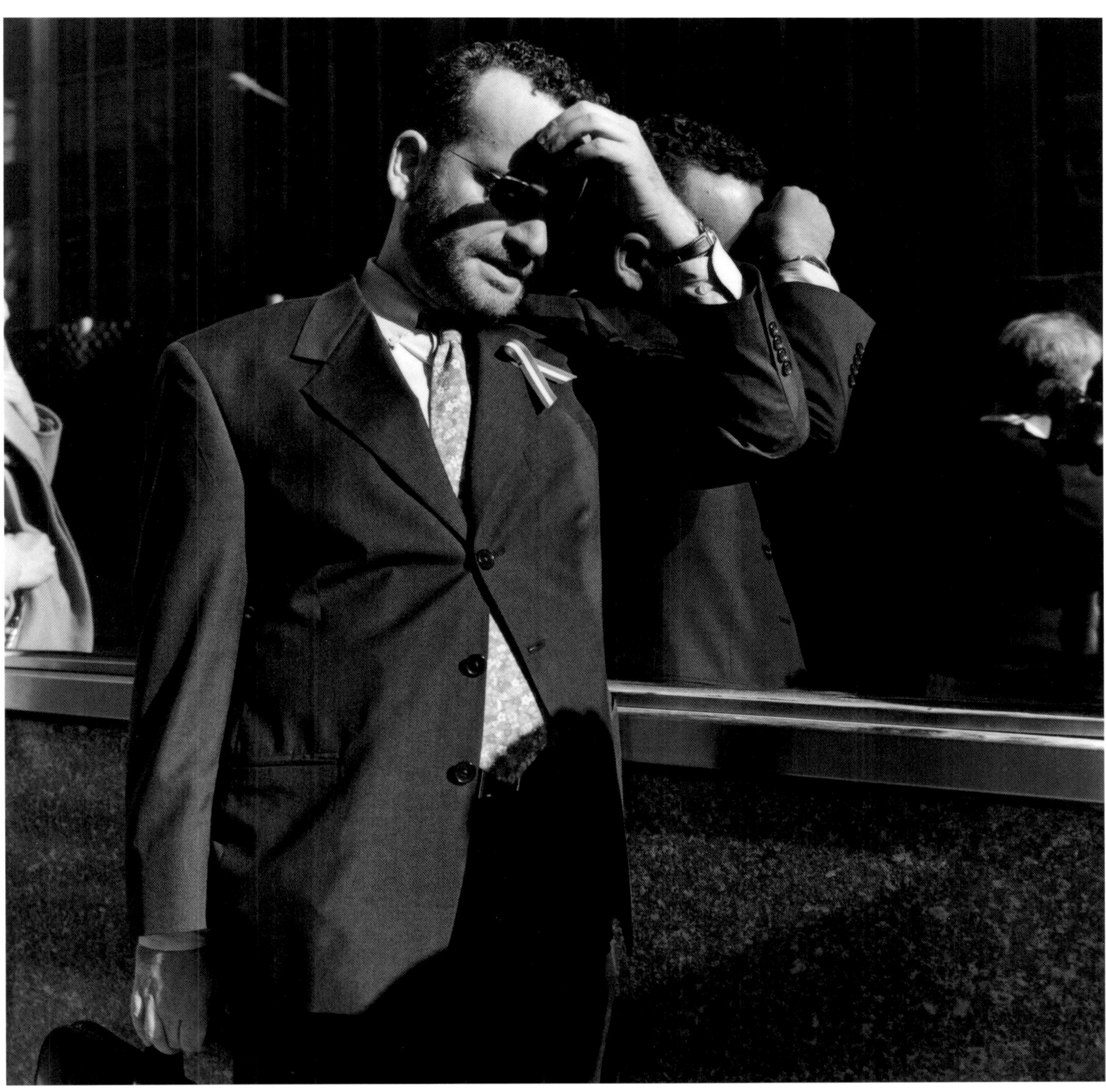

PILGRIMAGE

I made five trips to the World Trade Center site from my home in Vermont. I undertook the first trip two weeks after the attack. The last one took place December 19, 2001. I felt the need to witness and understand the impact of the New York City tragedy through my camera.

At the barricades surrounding the site, I found people experiencing a remarkable sense of community, but also the deepest kind of pesonal reflection on loss and mortality. I realized I was one of many who needed to be at the site, unable to grasp the terrible television, magazine, and newspaper images. Men in suits, teenaged friends, families, young lovers, tourists, visitors from around the world, and fathers with children on their shoulders: all slowly approached the site. Eventually they came to a full stop, planting their feet firmly as if to keep themselves from wavering or falling. Then each visitor's quiet moment of reflection began as he or she stared off at the awful, cascading ruin of twisted steel, steeped in a swirl of acidic smoke. In this silence most visitors appeared to finally grasp, visually, the horror.

–Kevin Bubriski
Shaftsbury, VT
December 2001

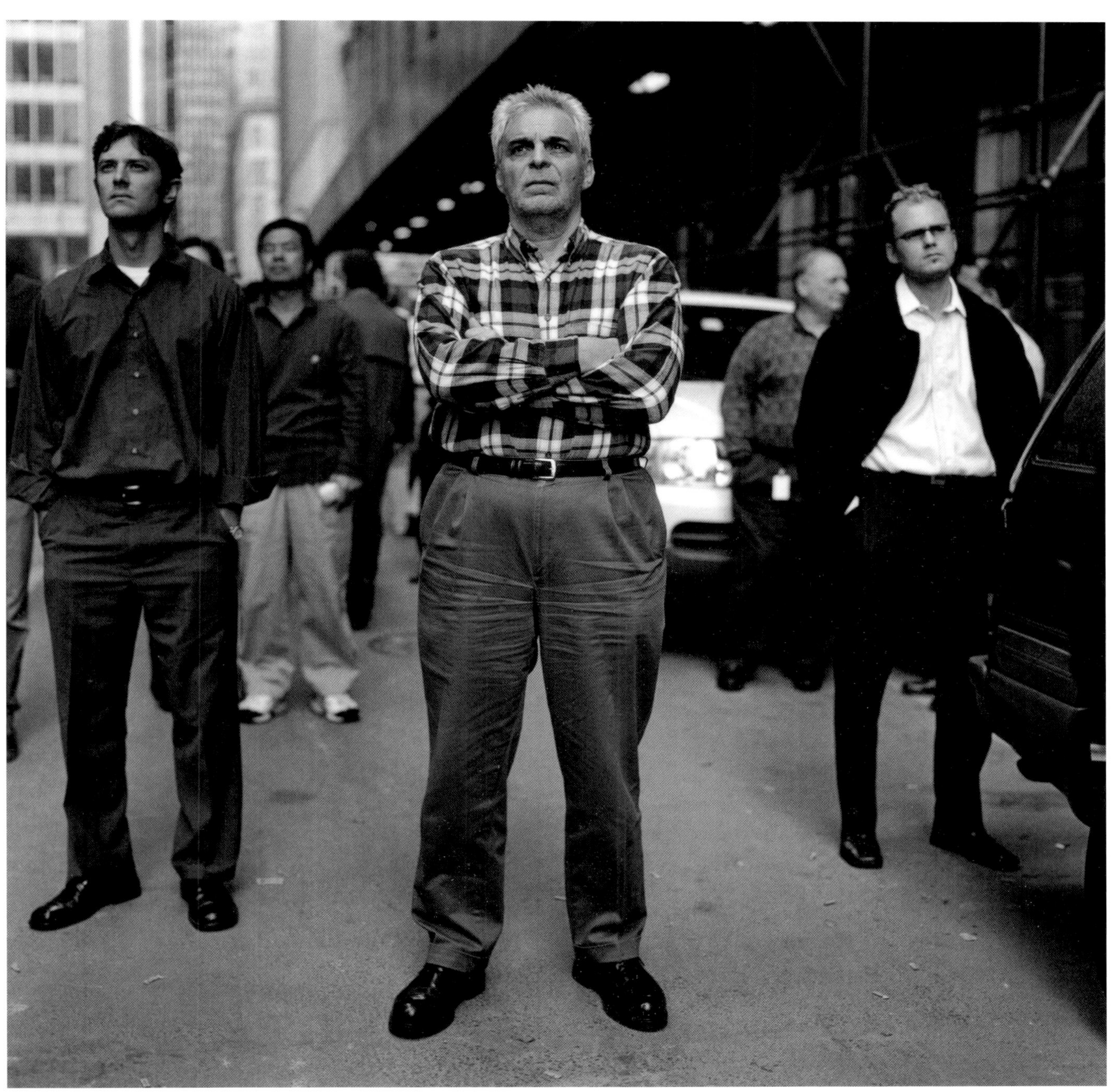

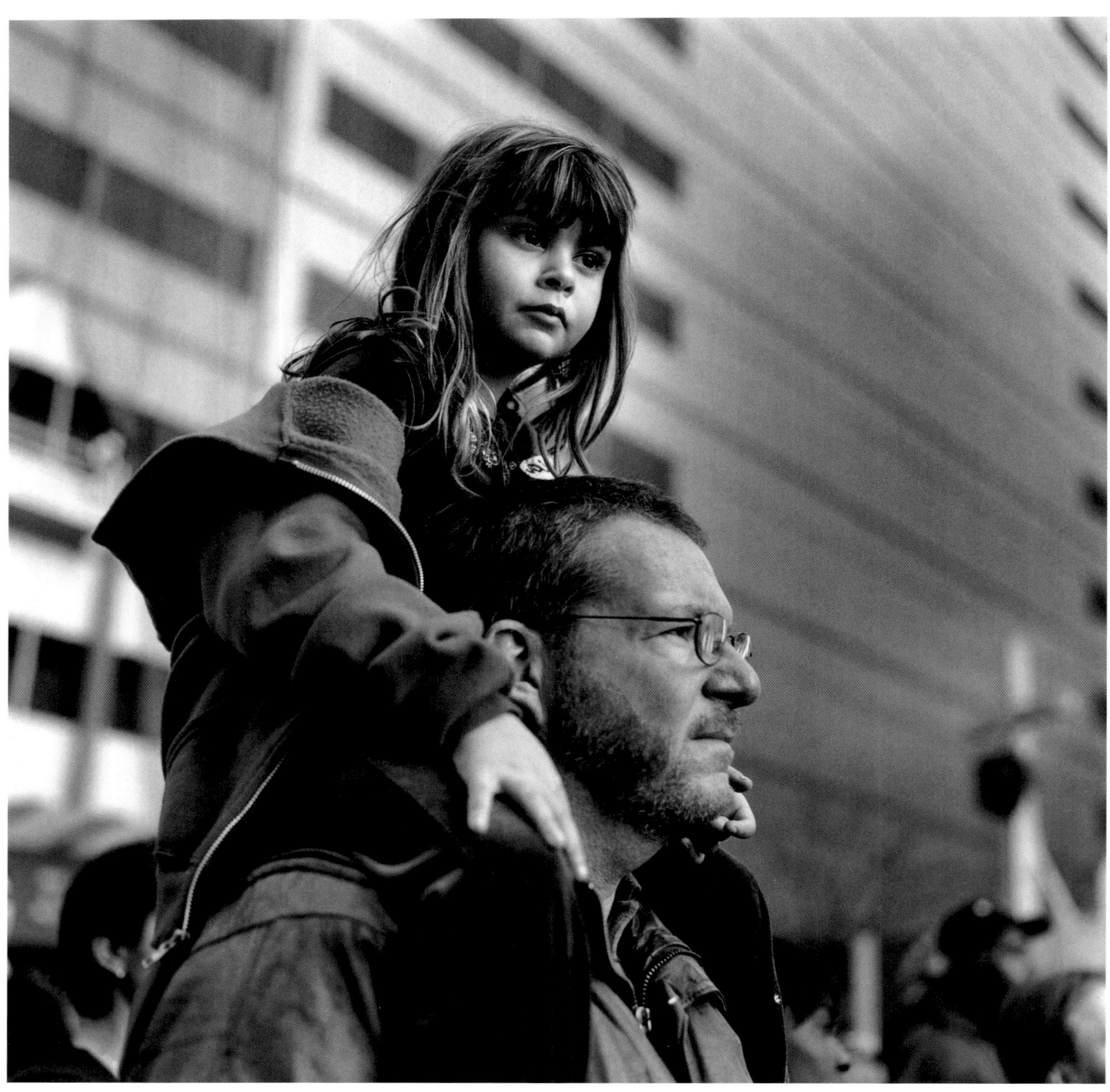

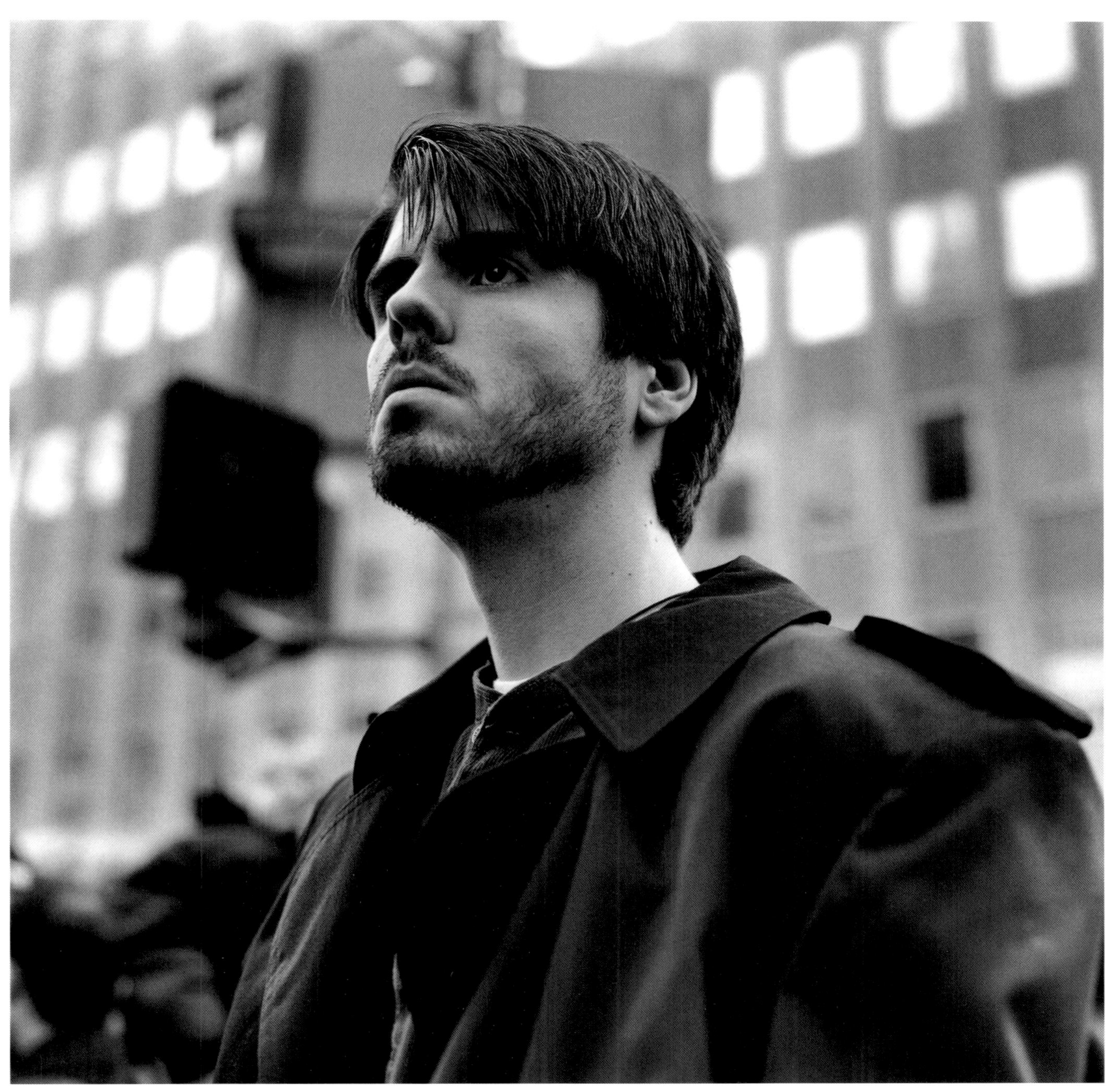

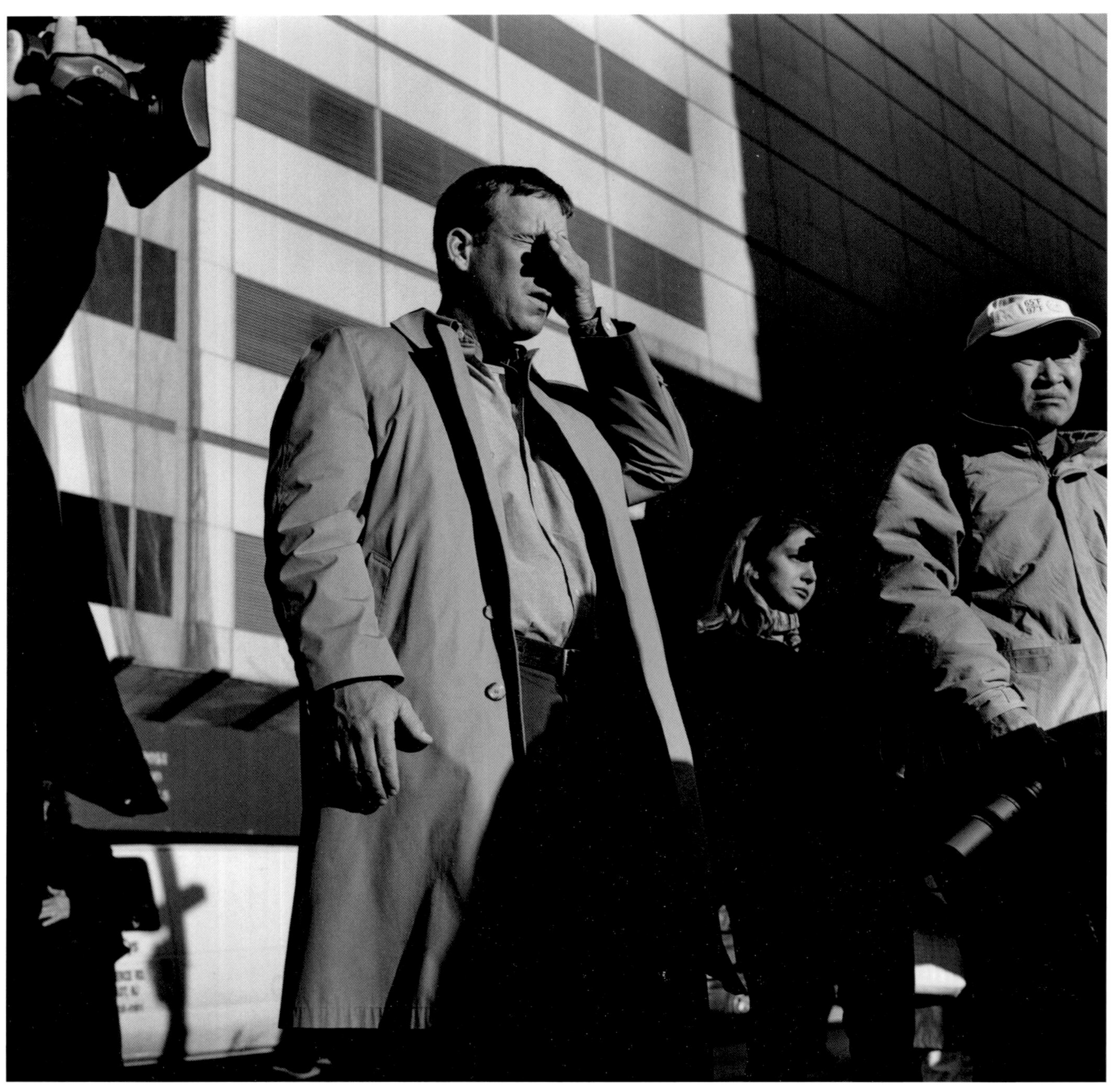

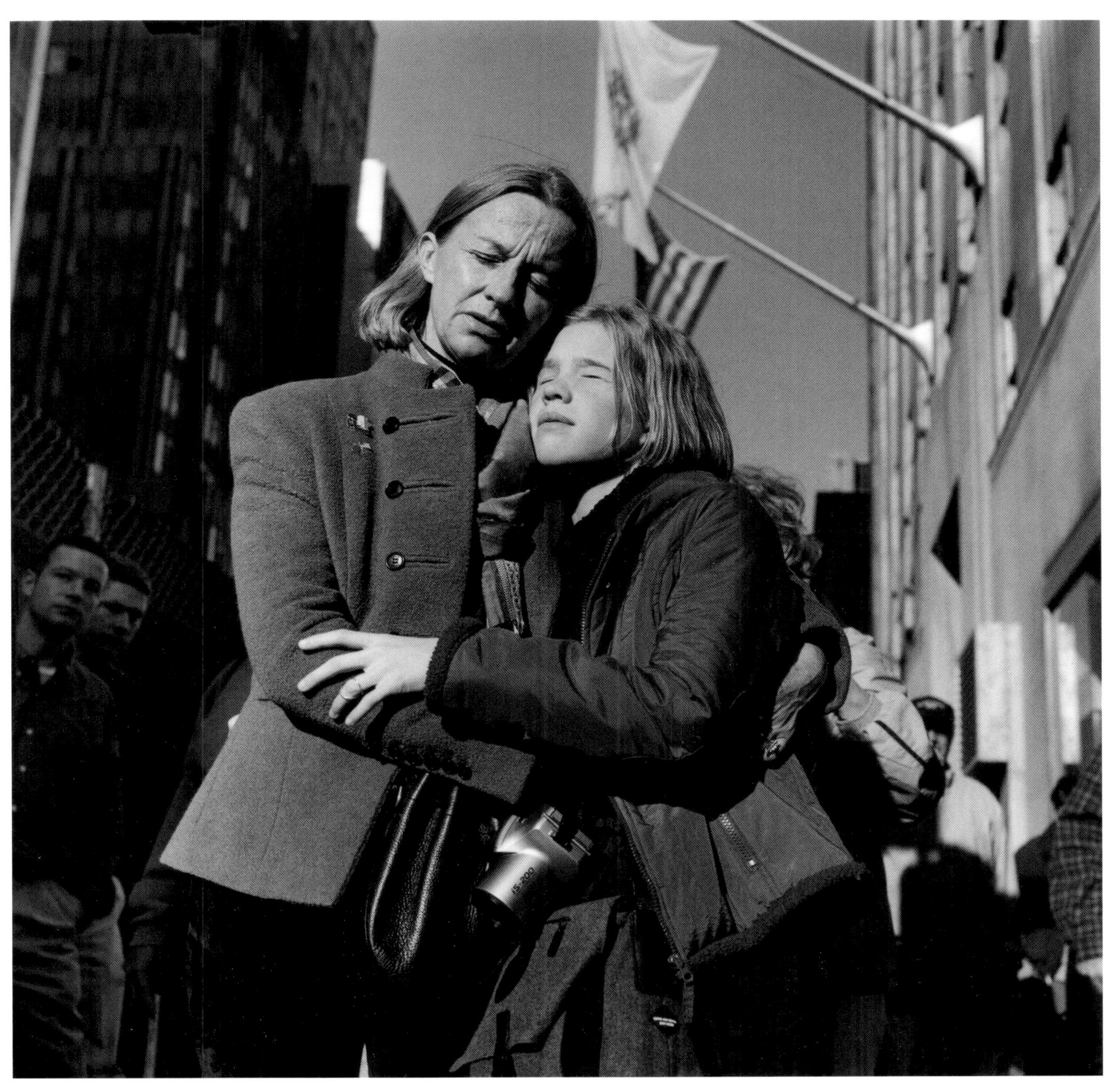

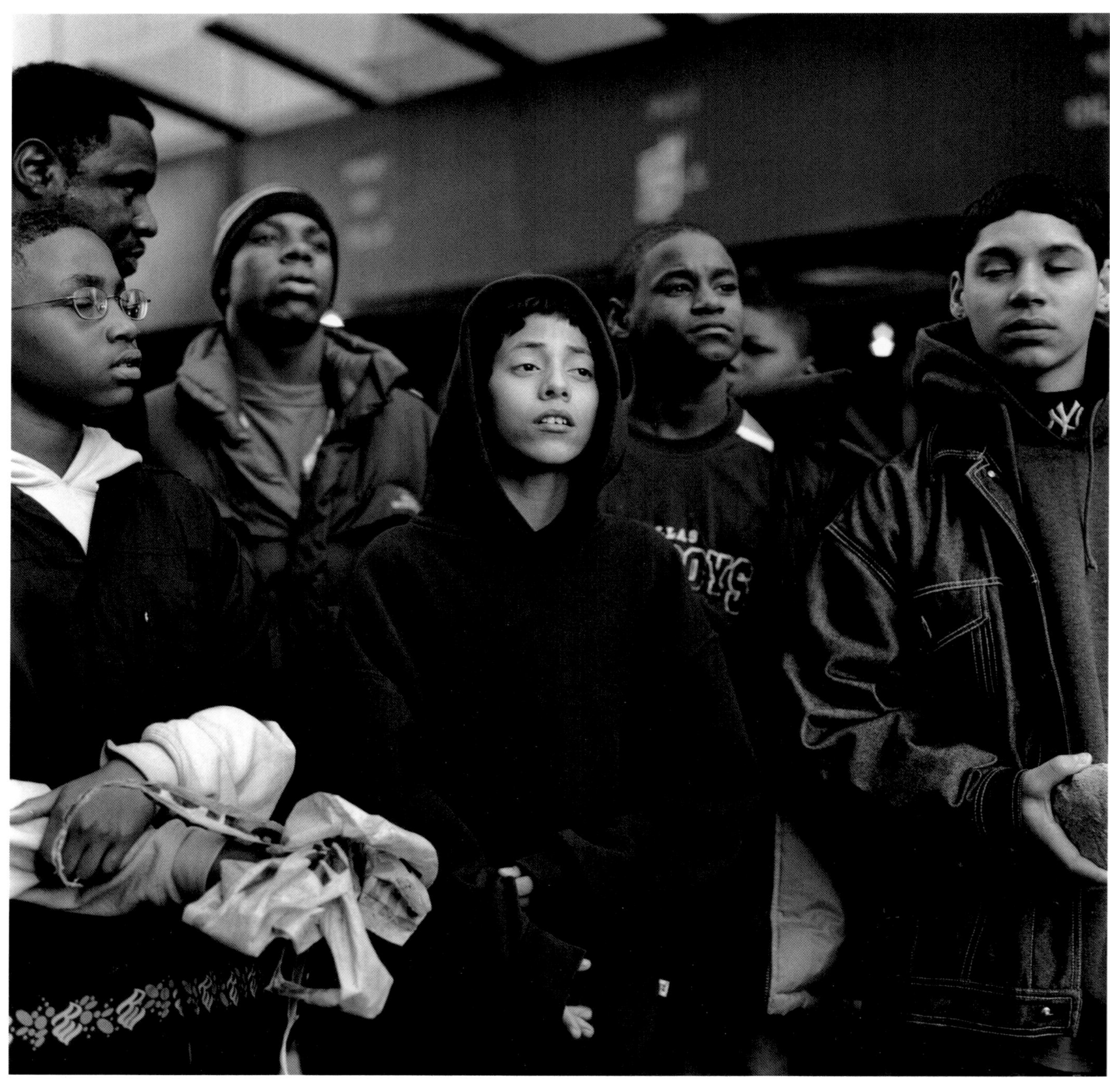

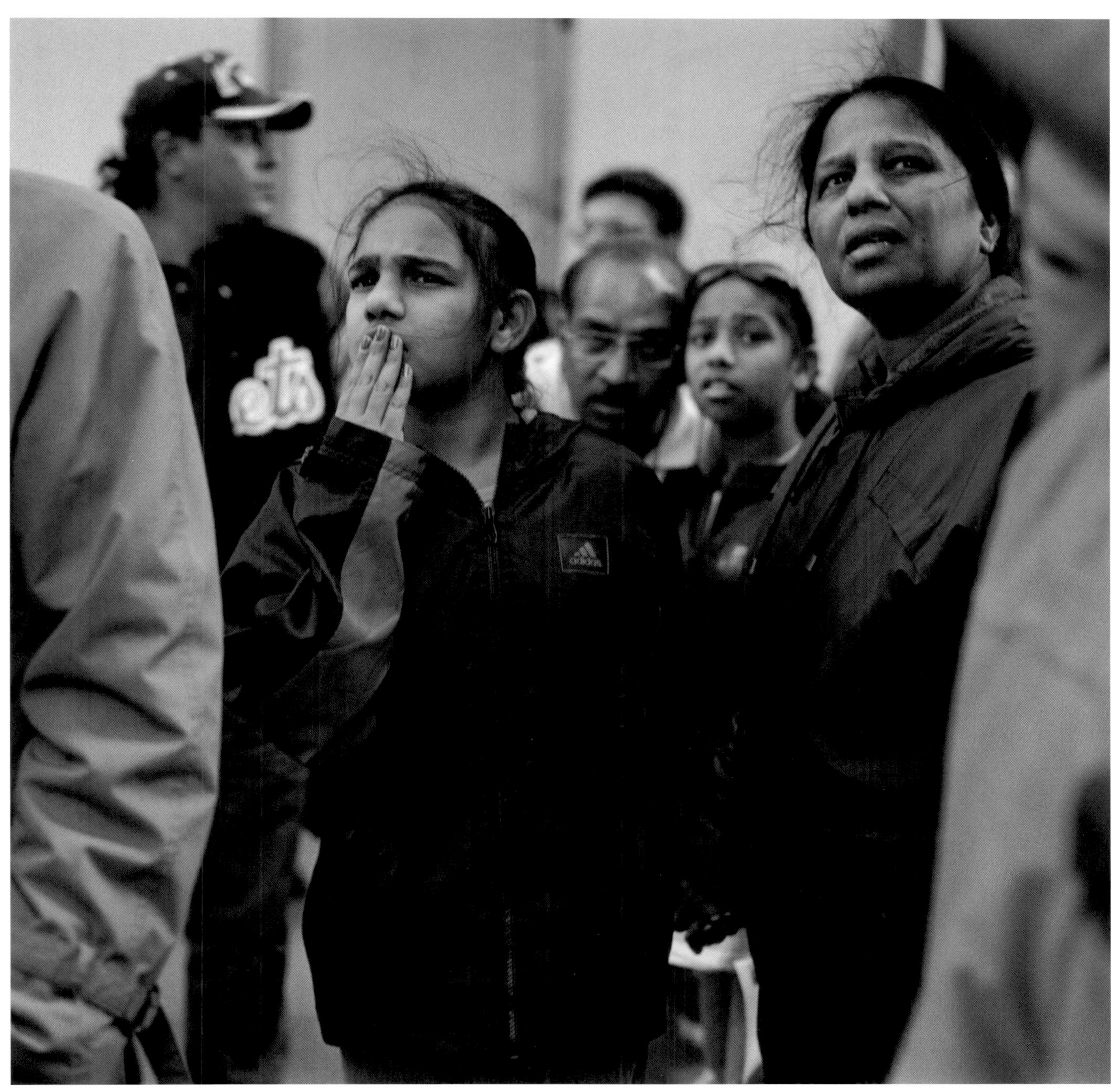

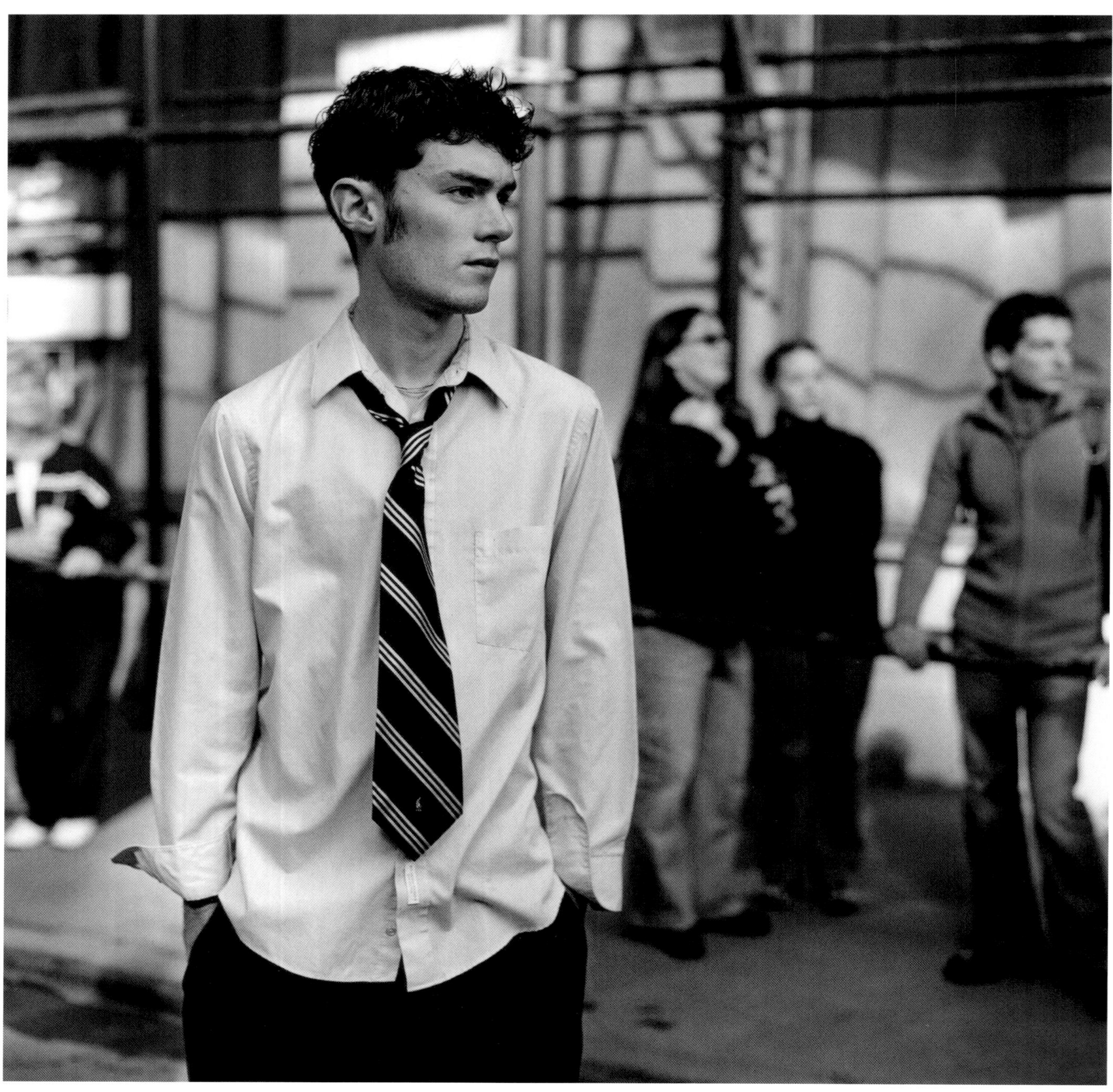

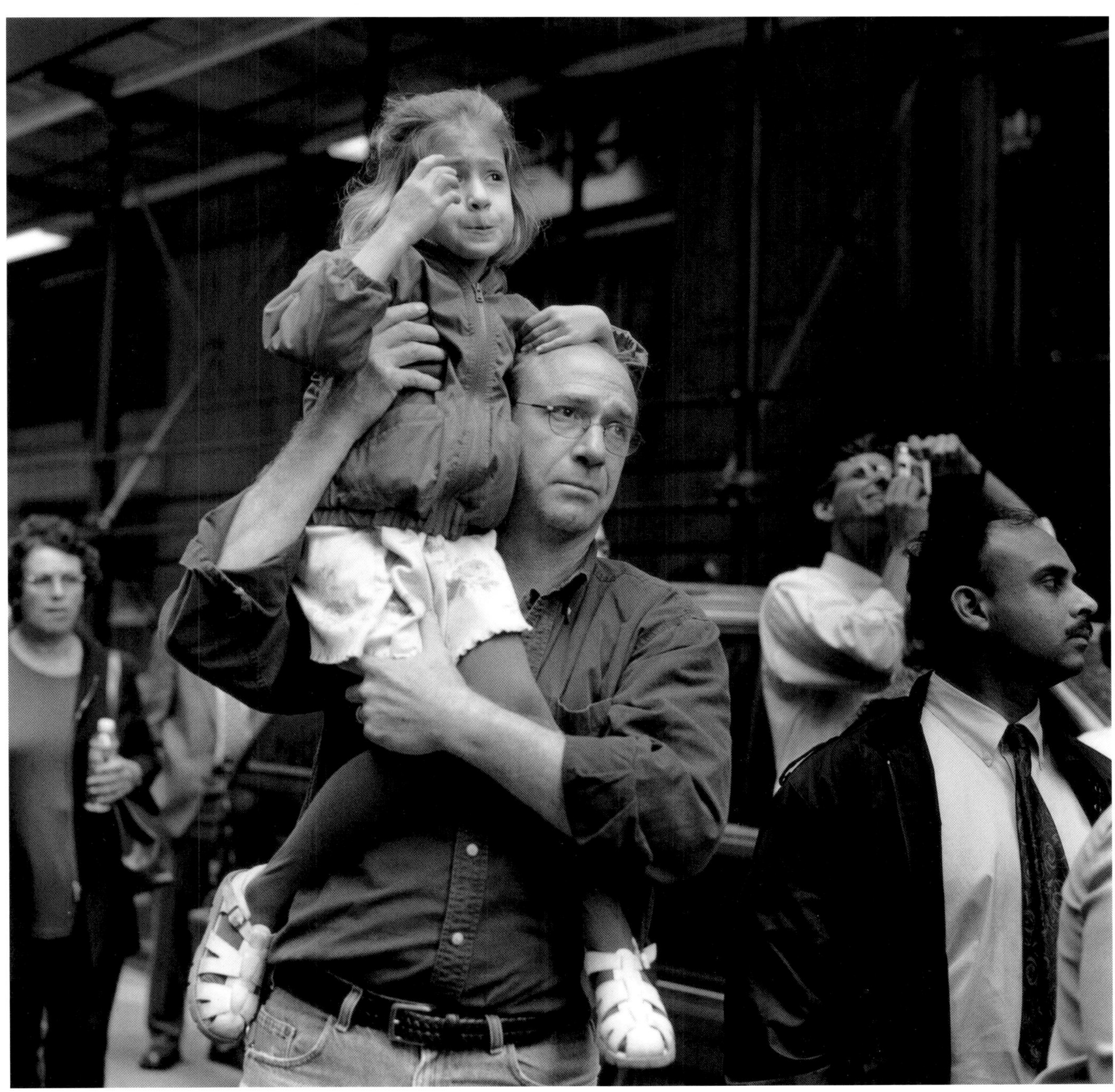

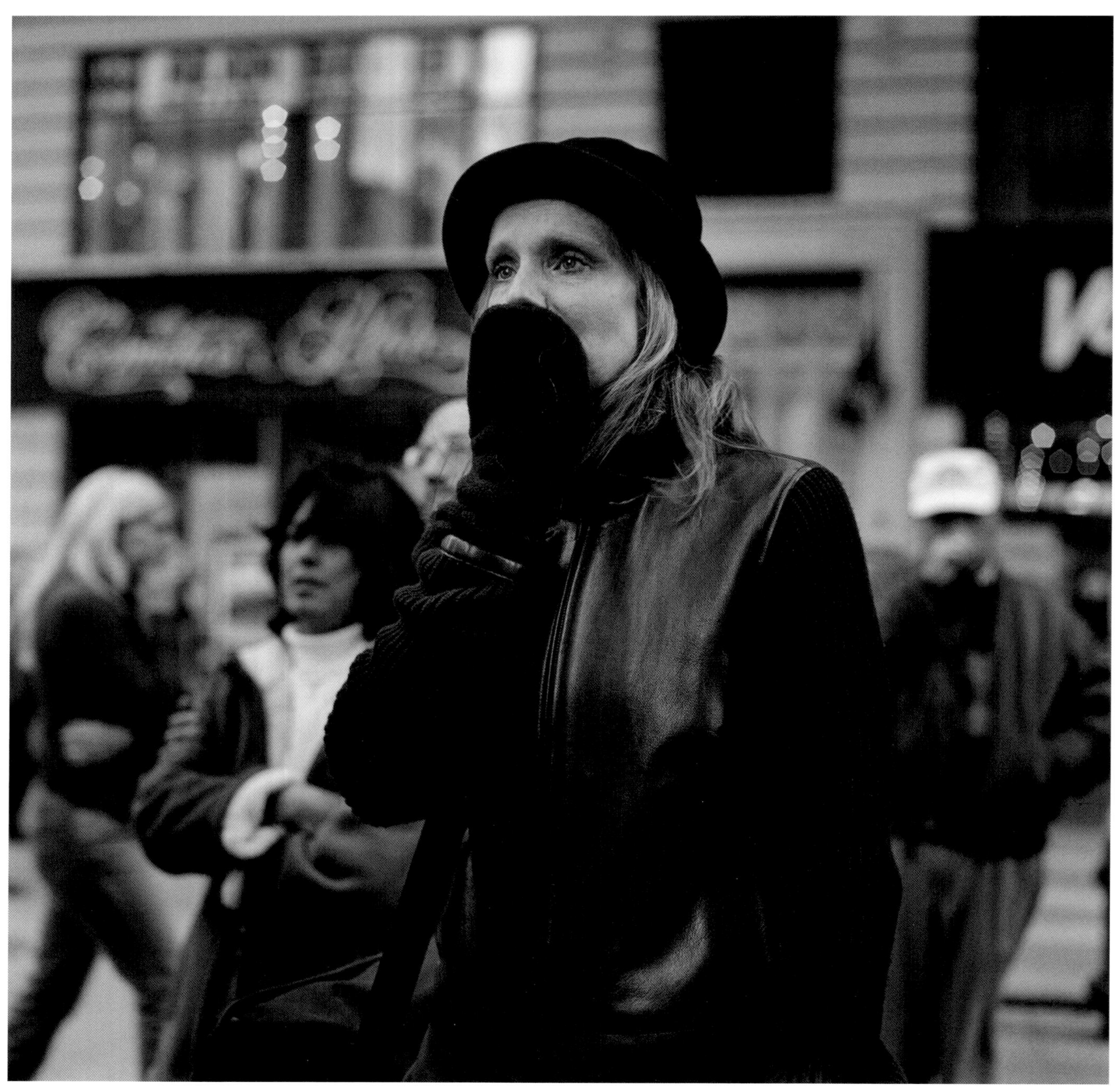

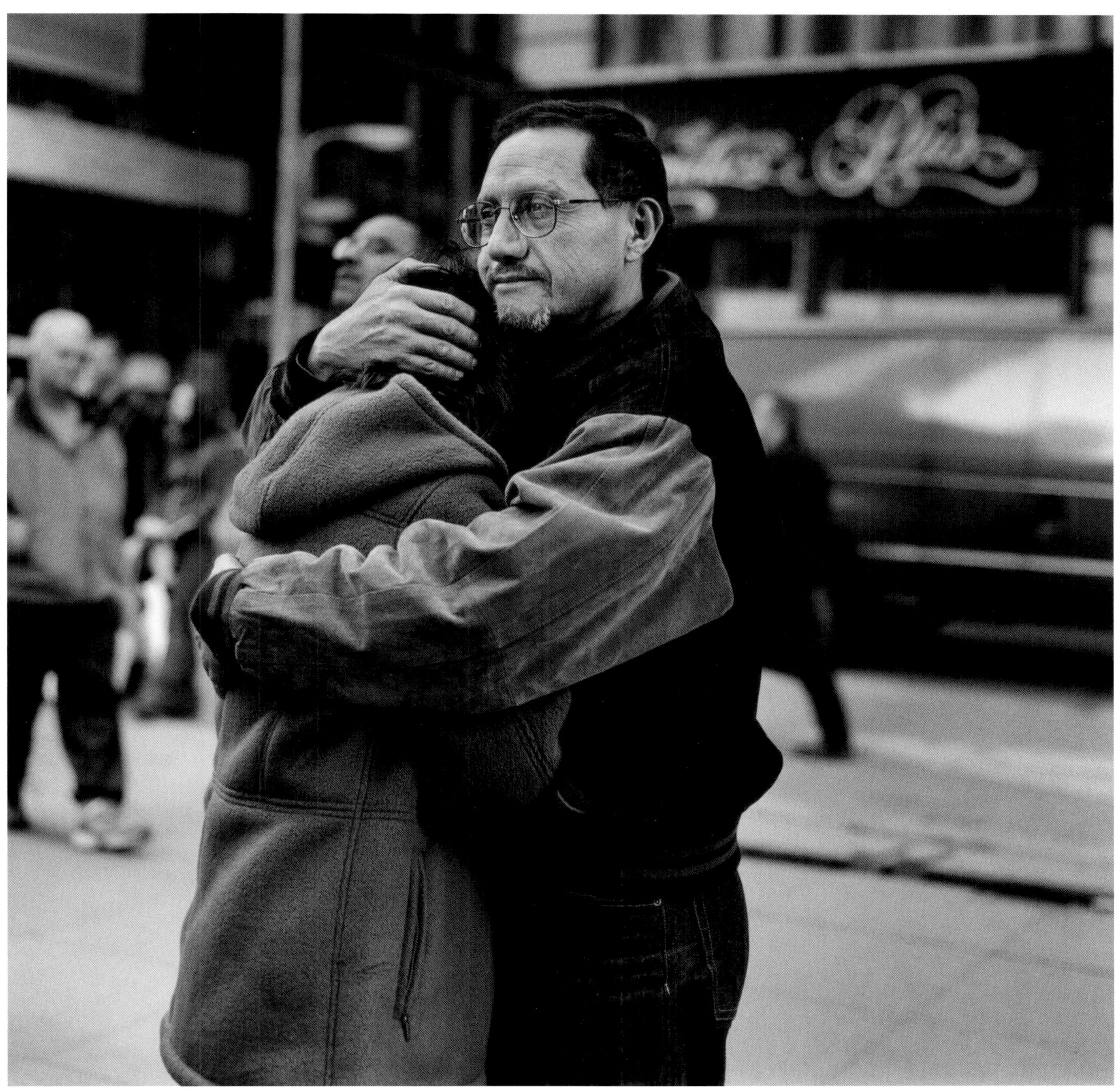

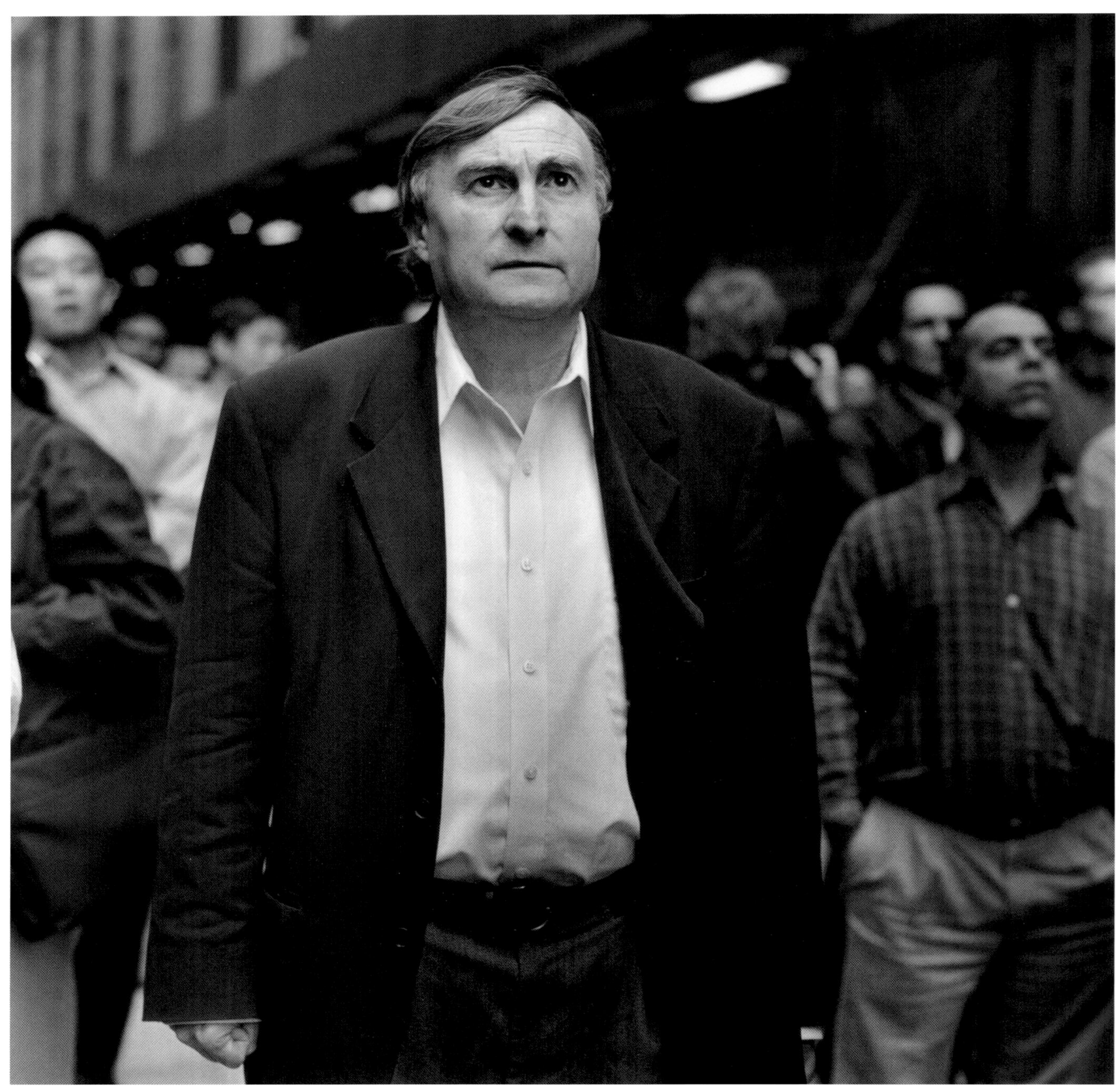

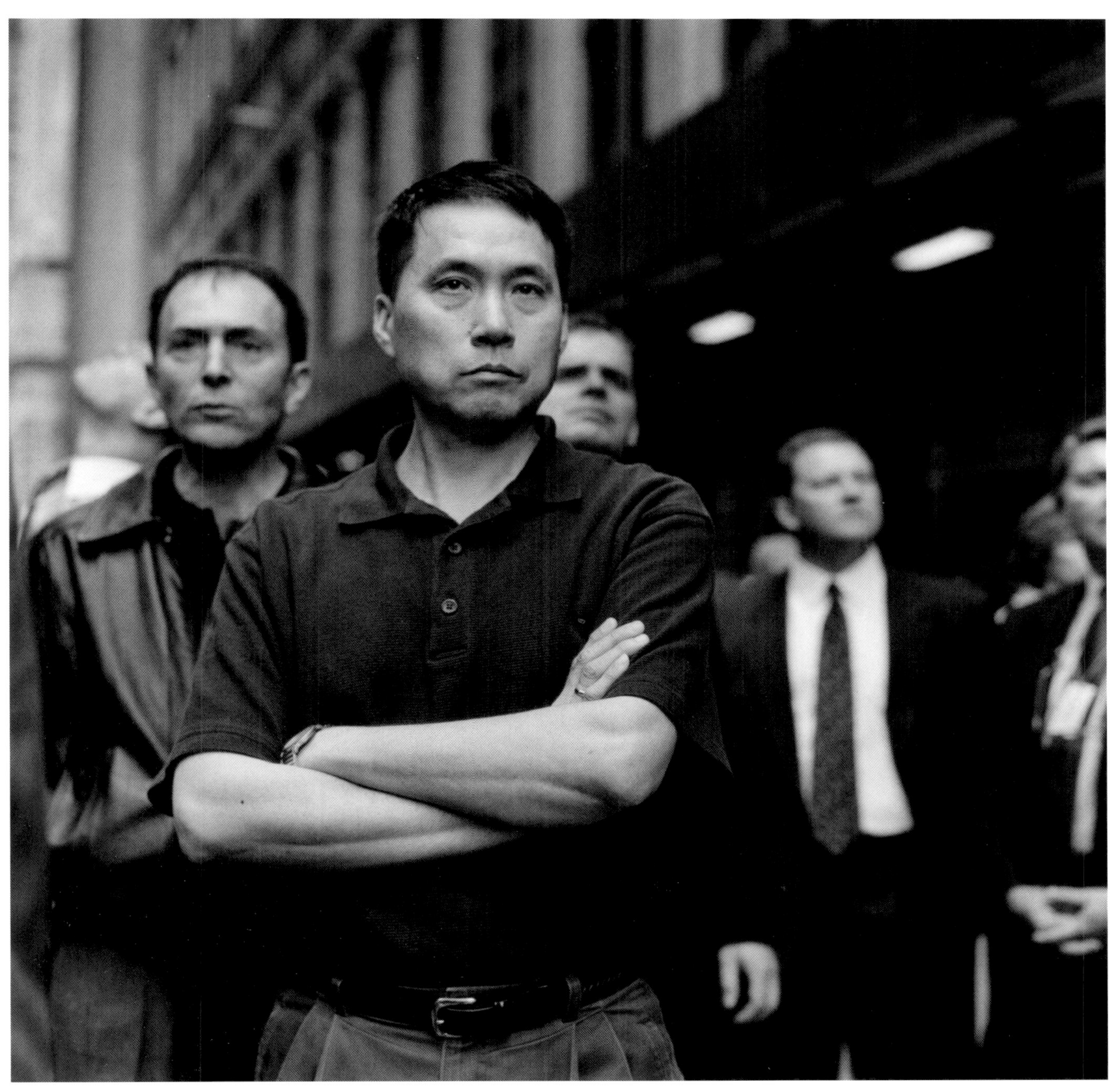

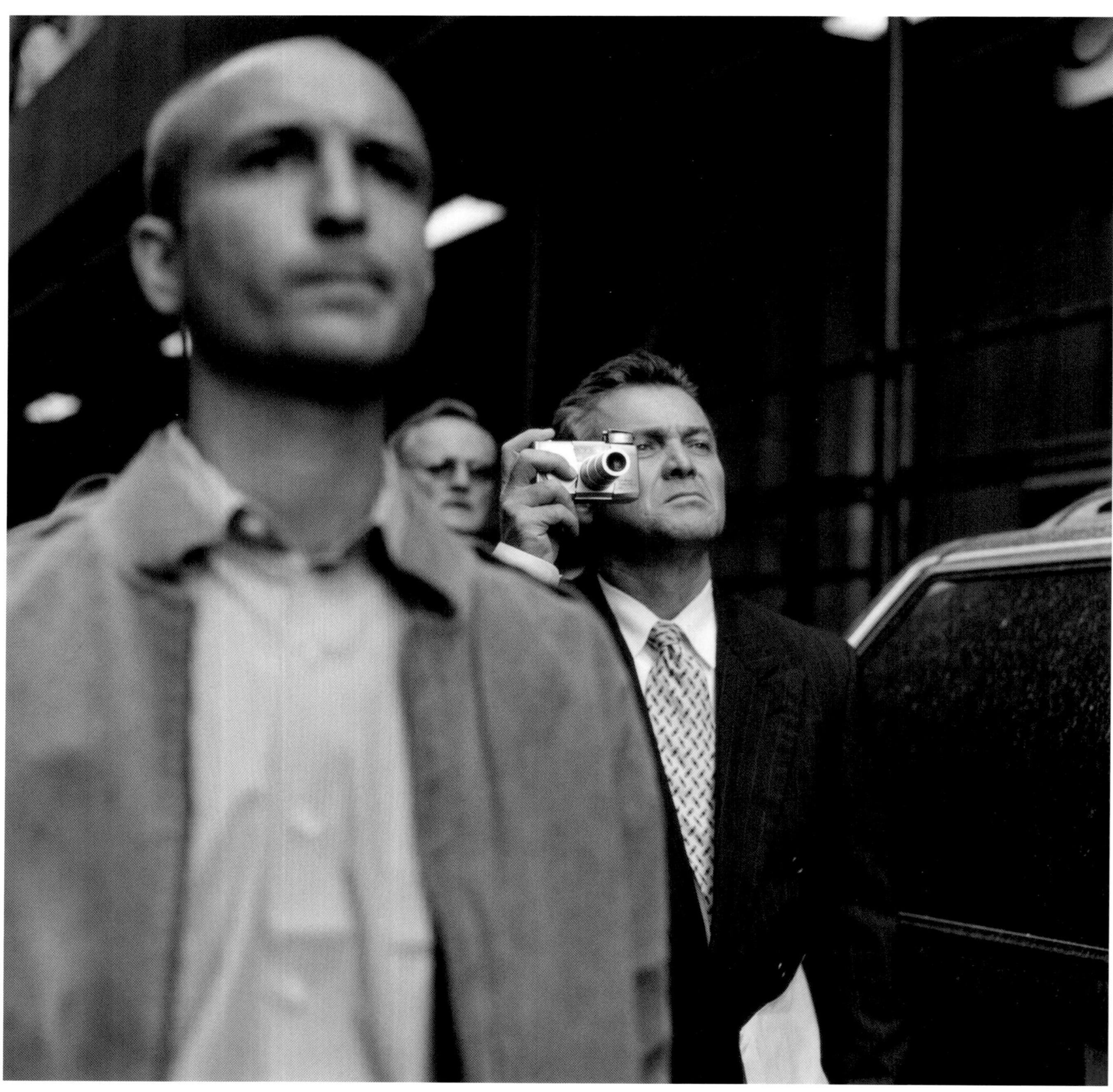

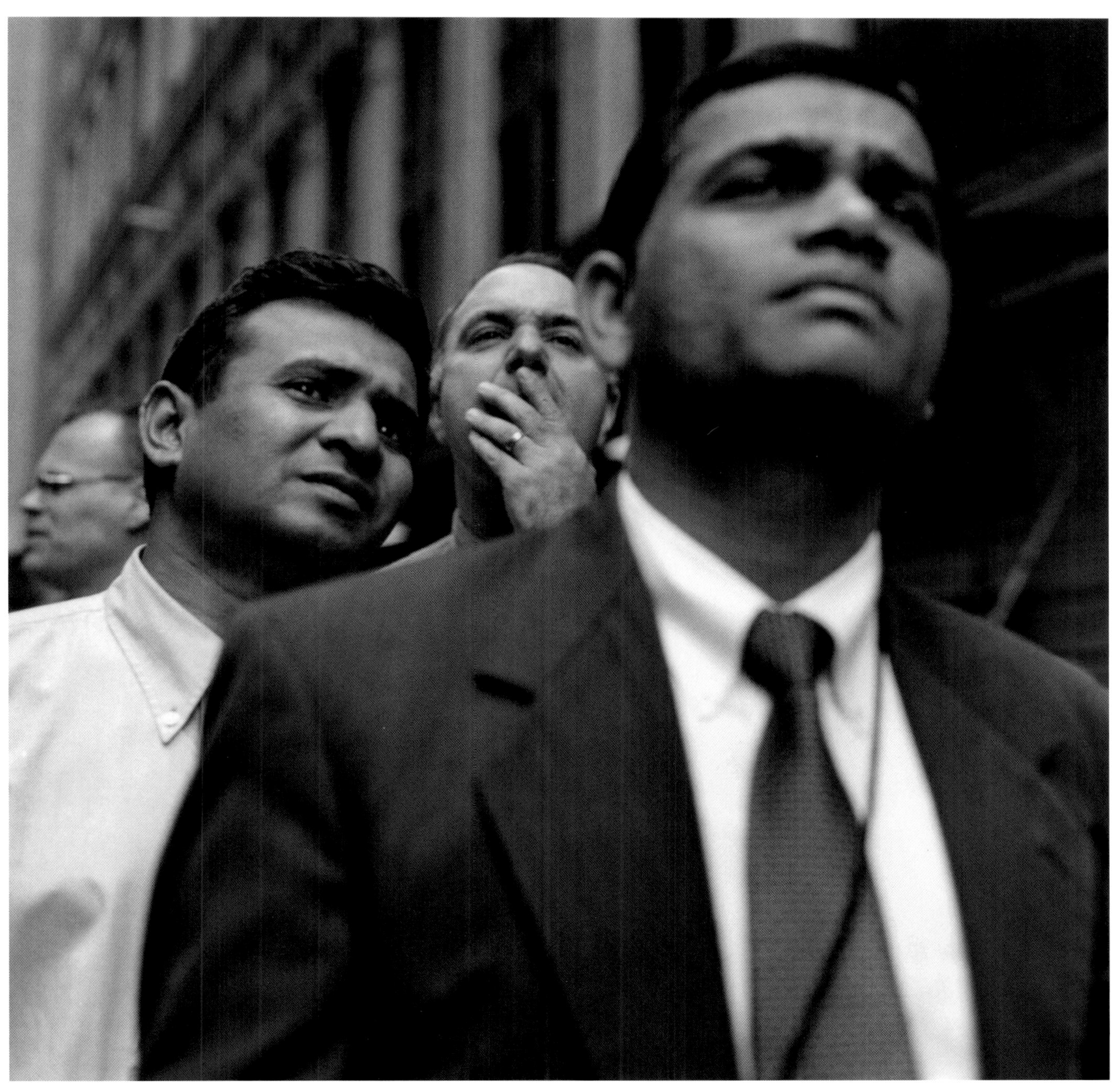

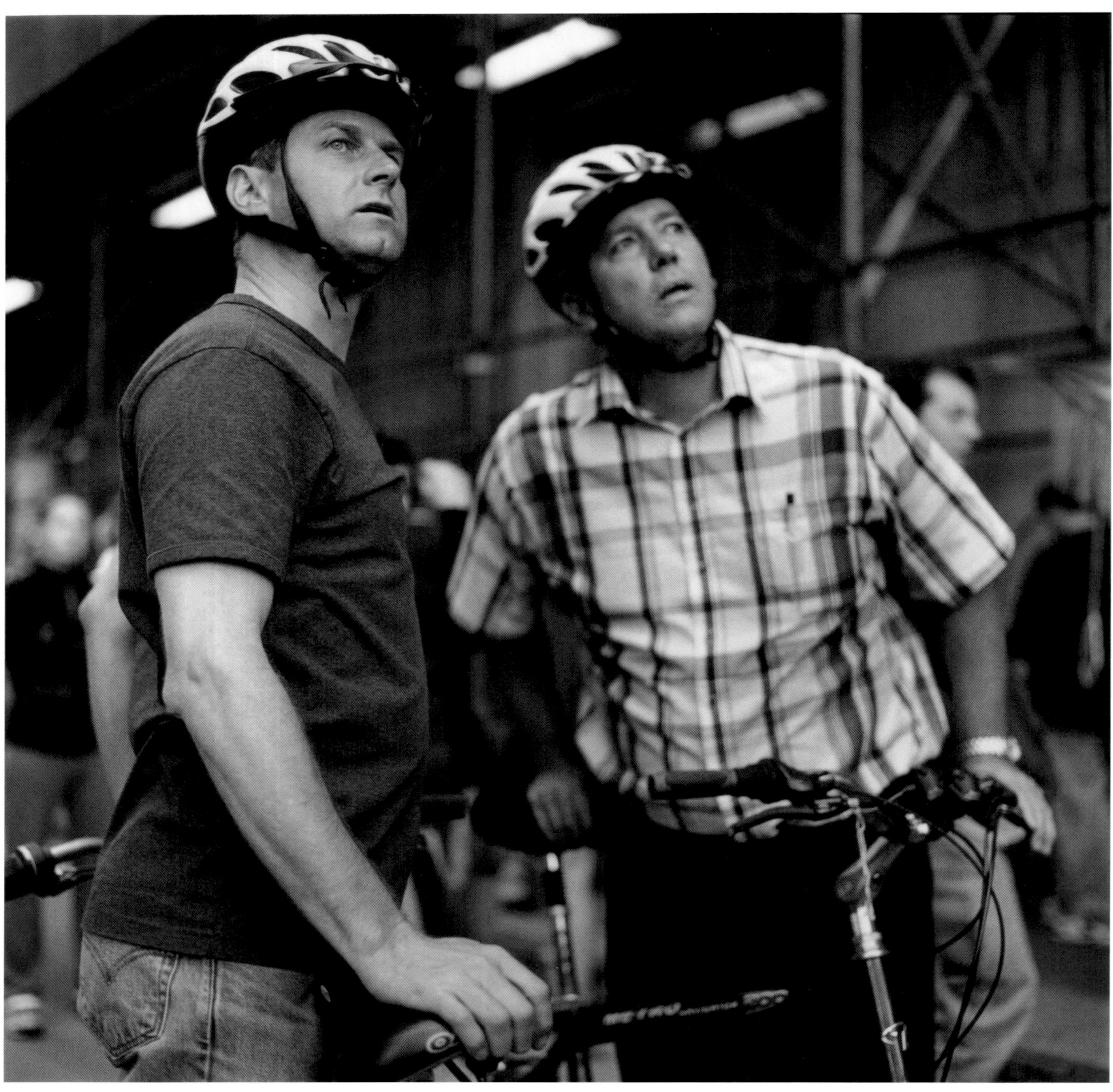

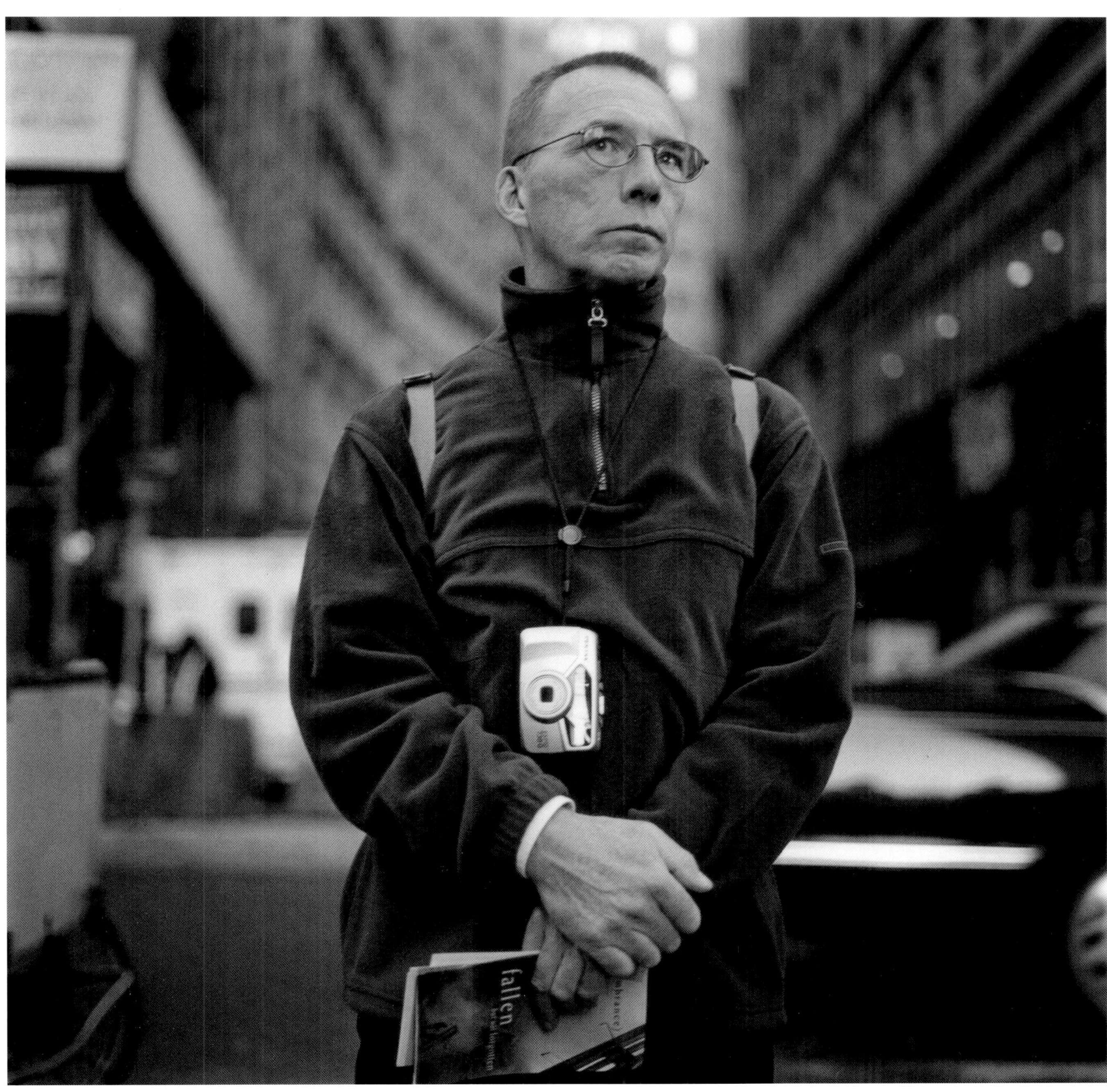
fallen

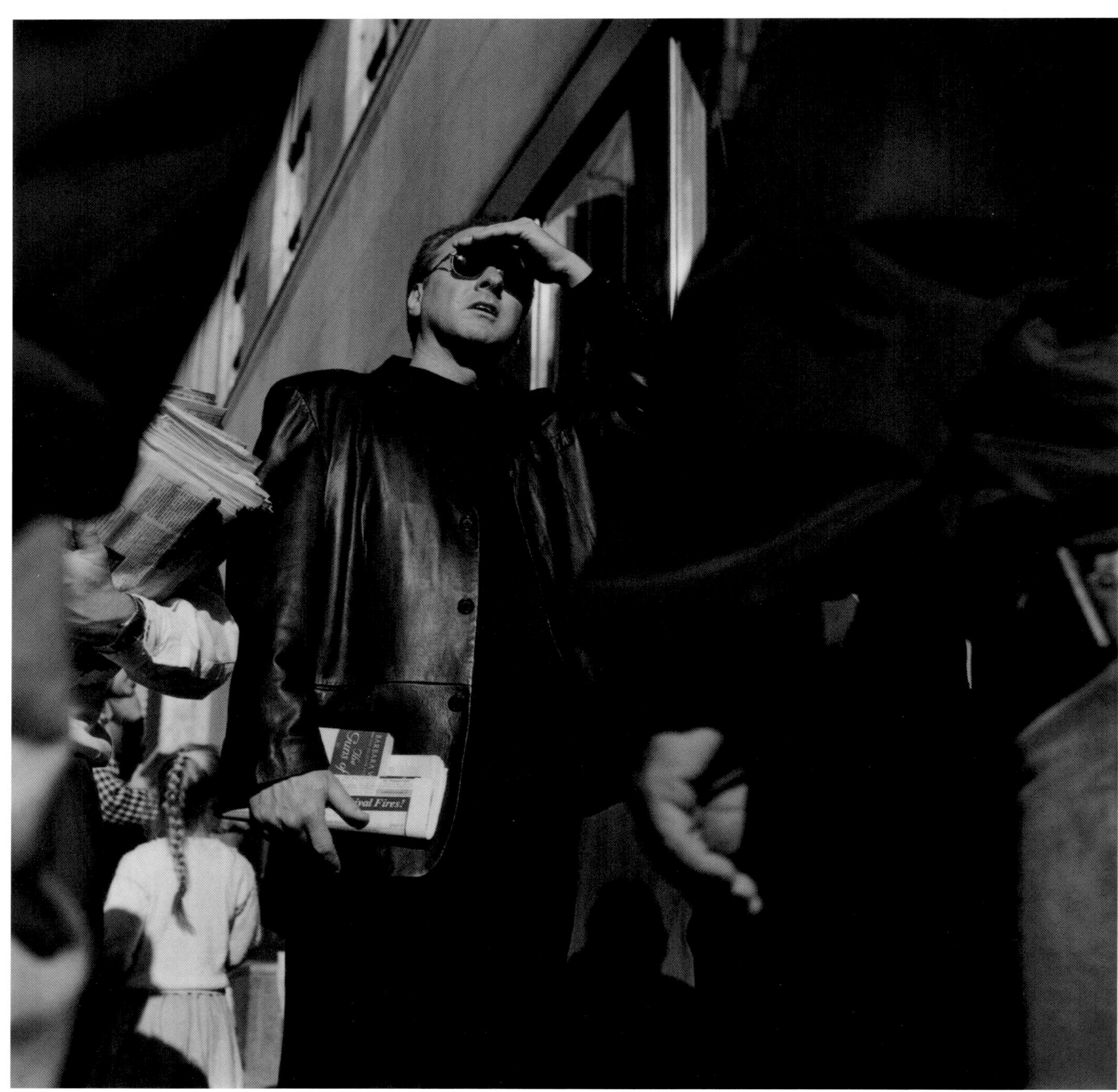

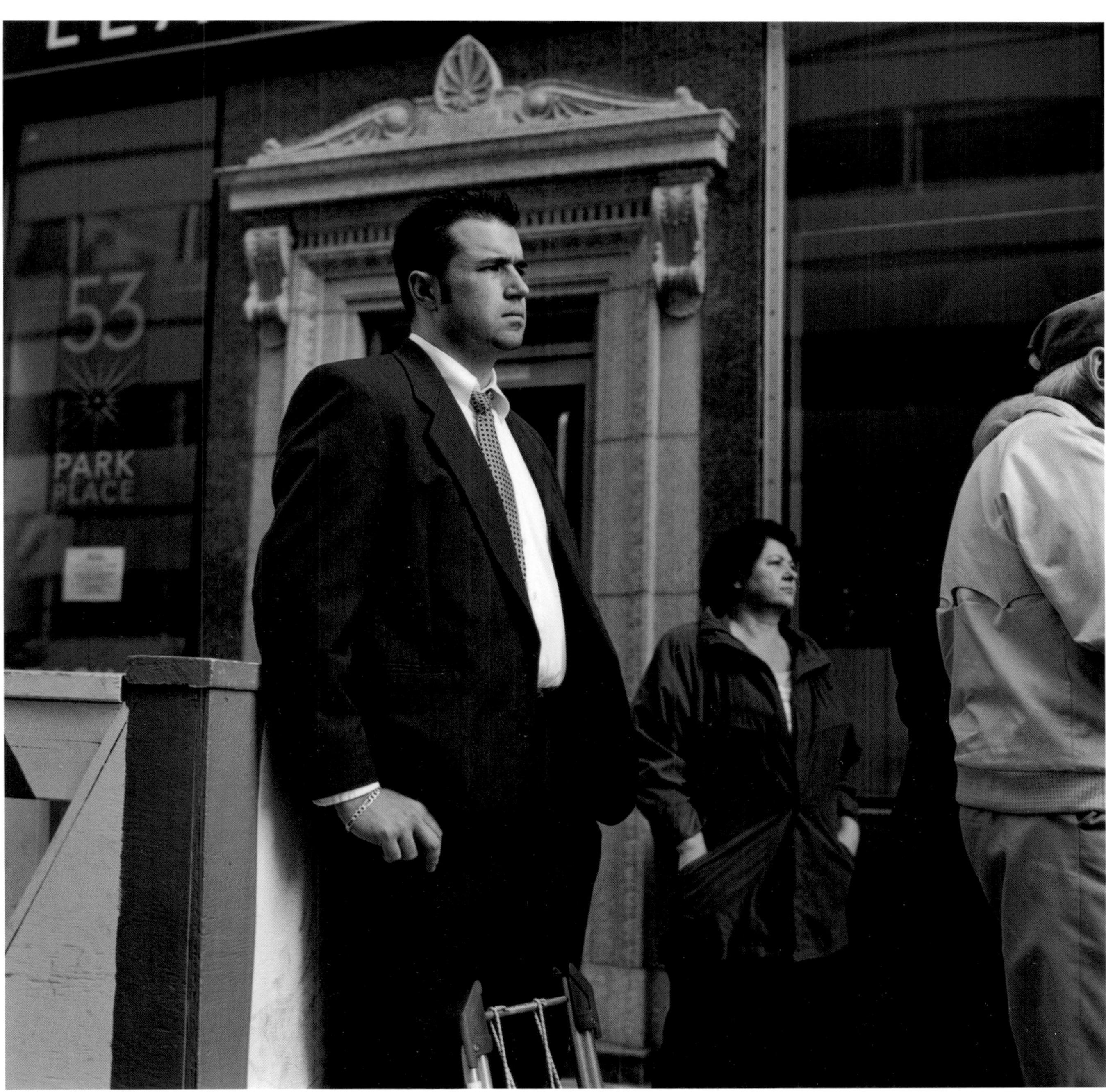
53
PARK
PLACE

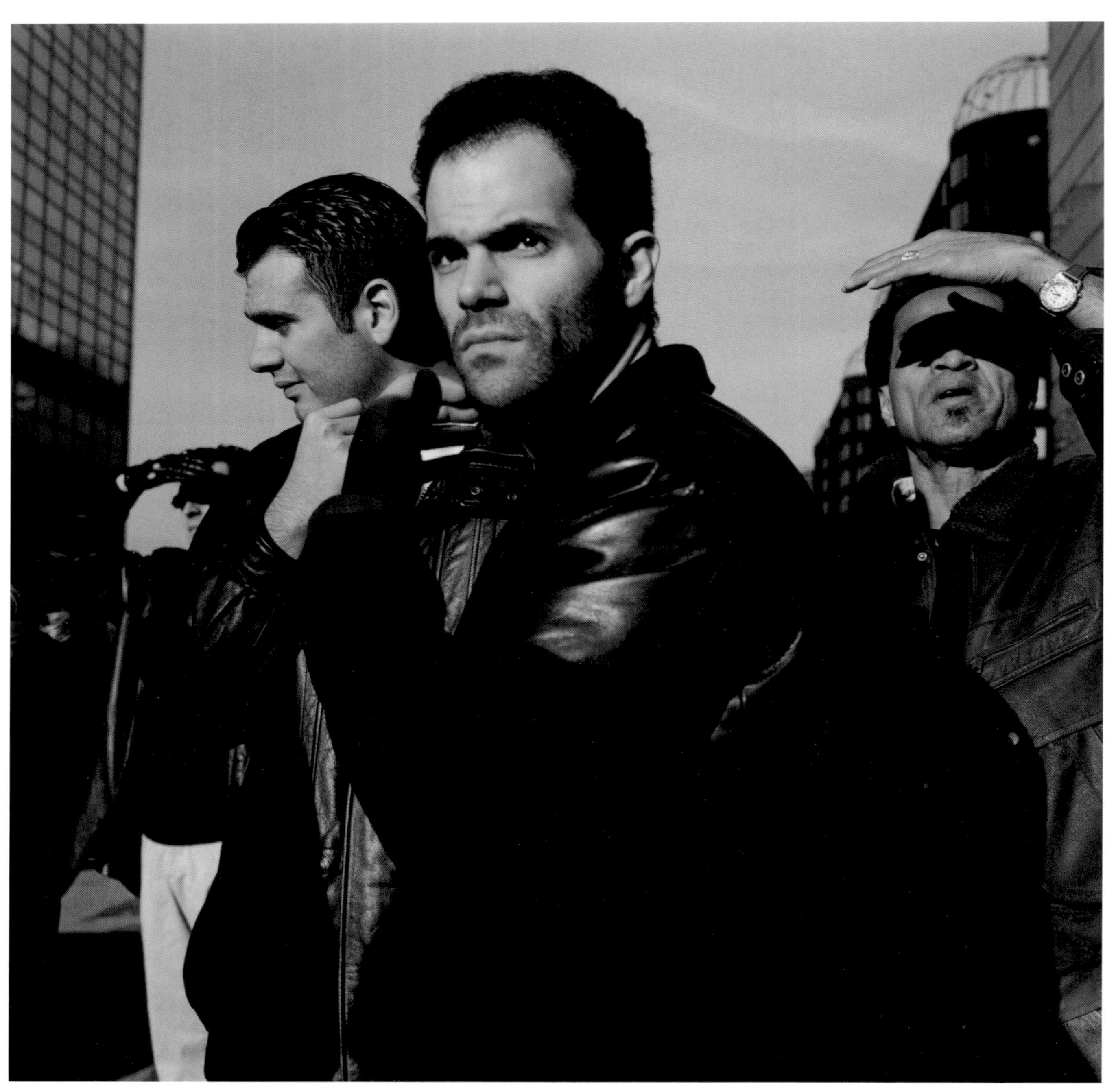

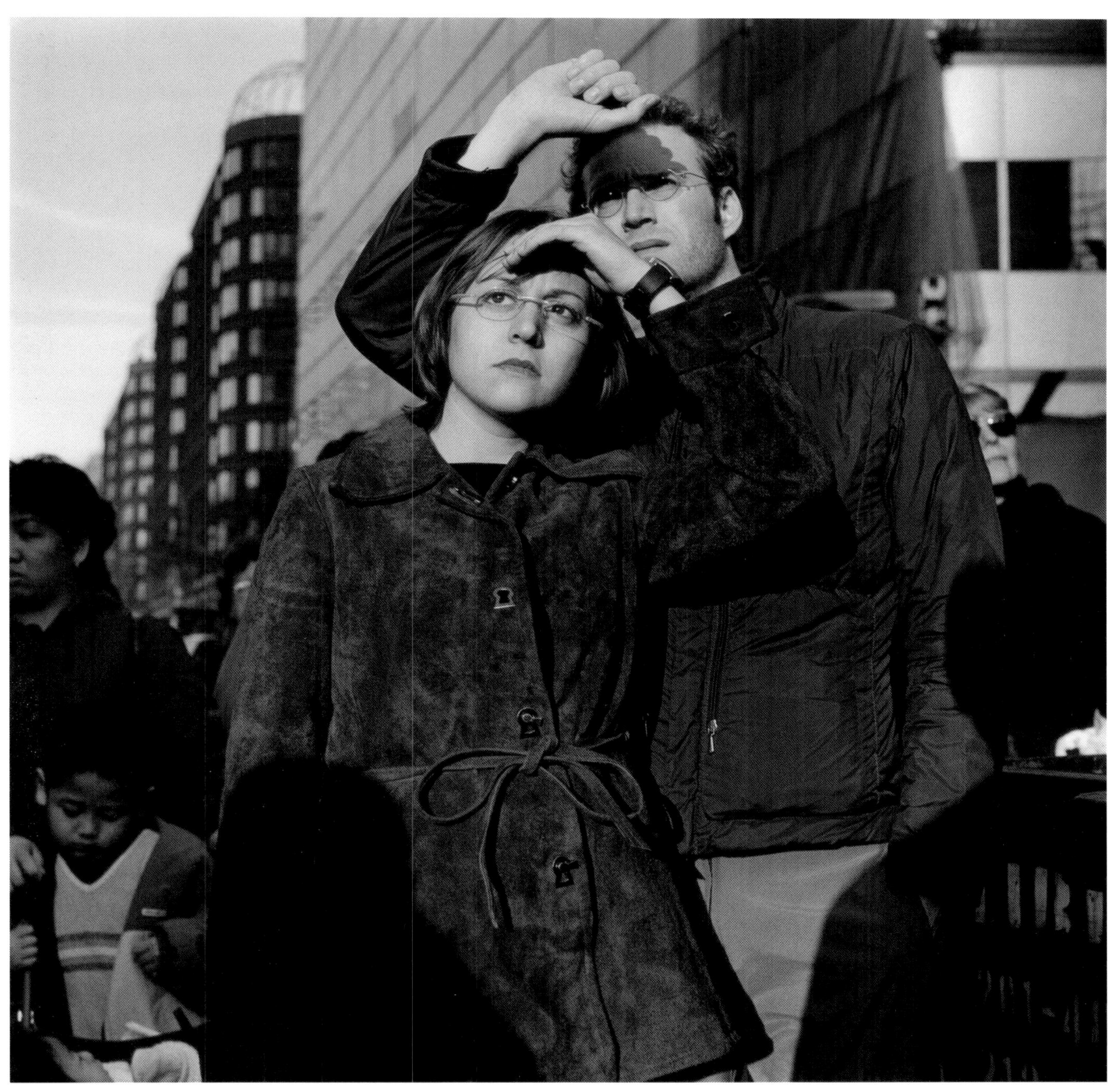

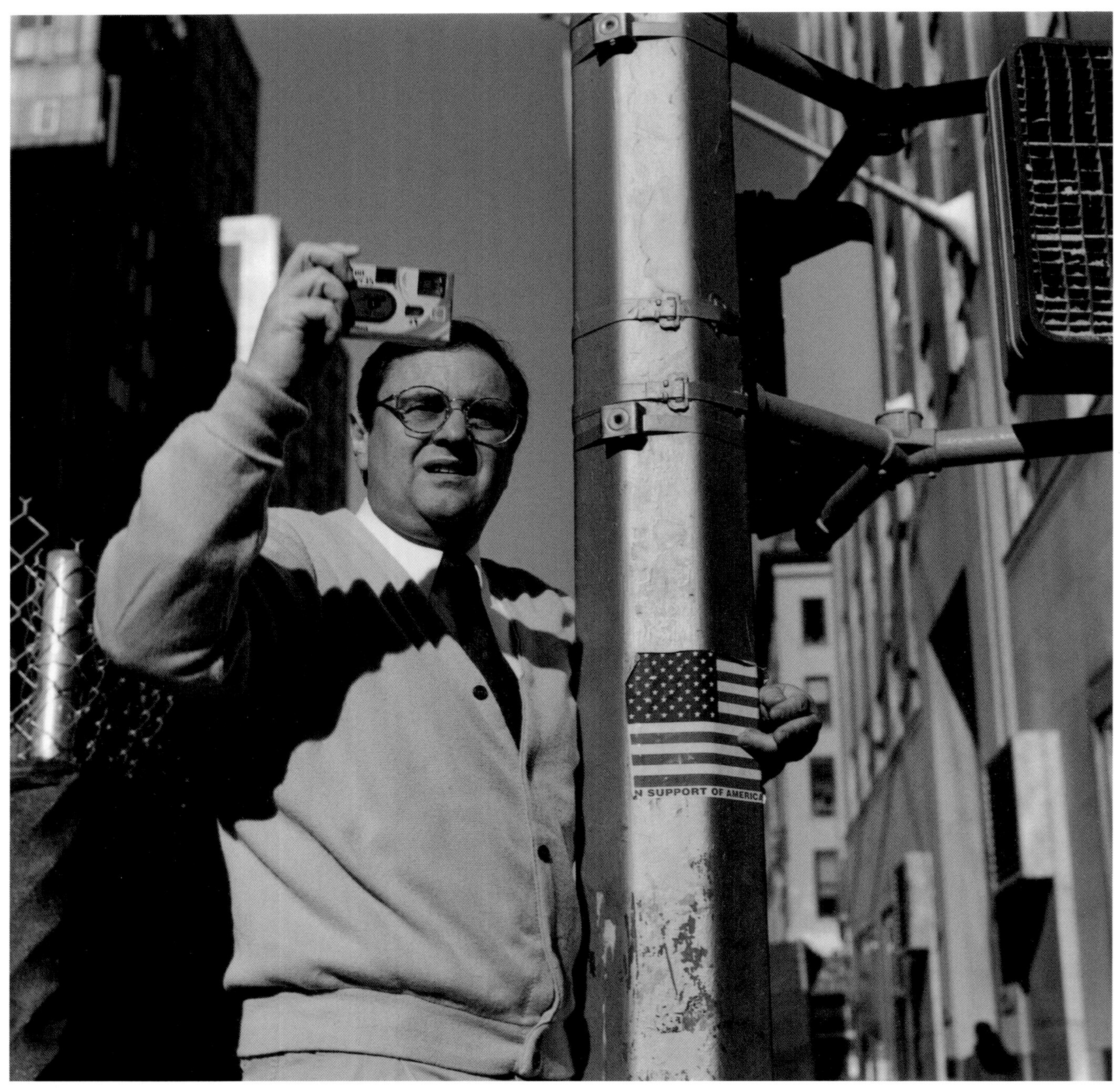
N SUPPORT OF AMERICA

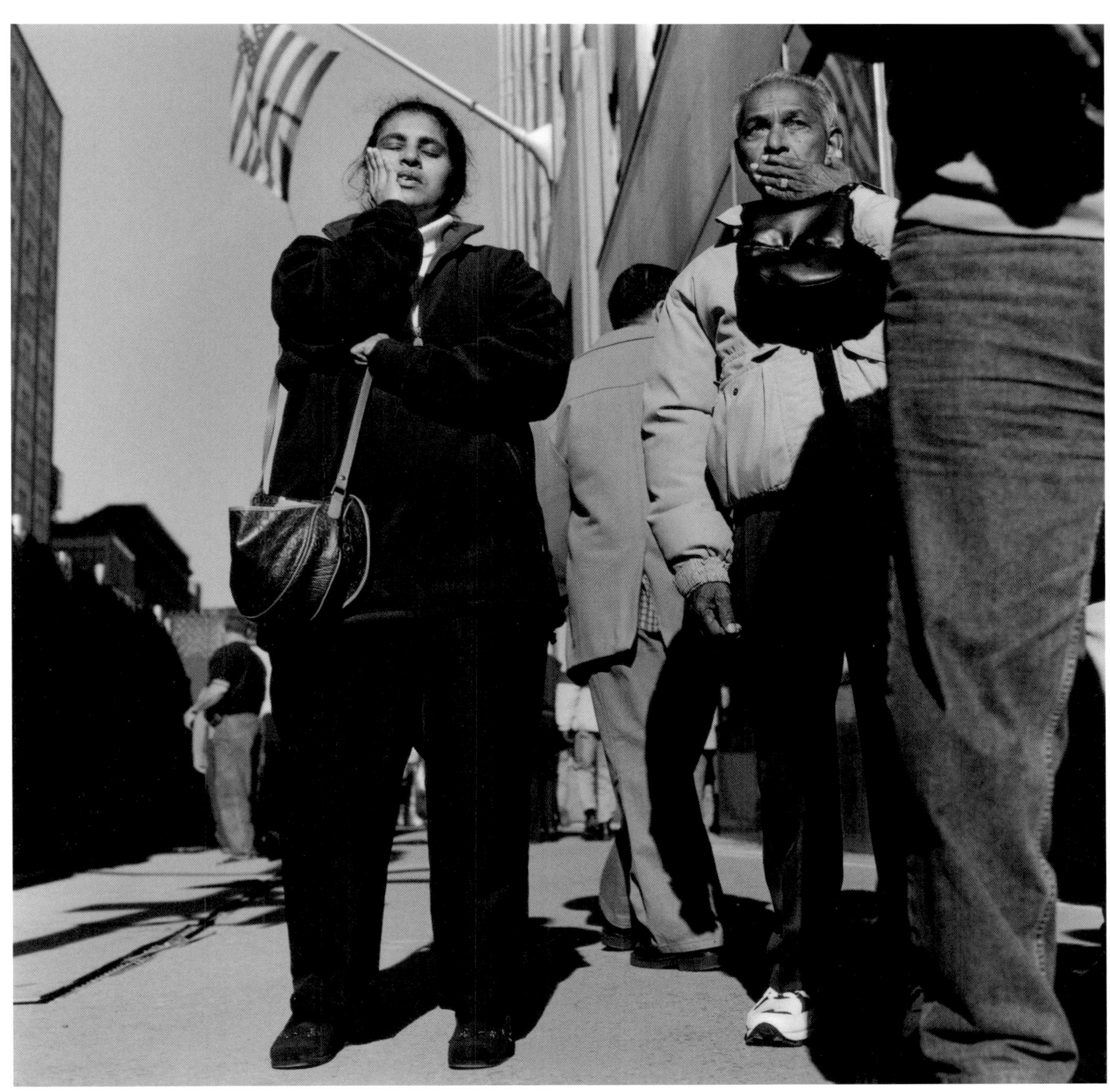

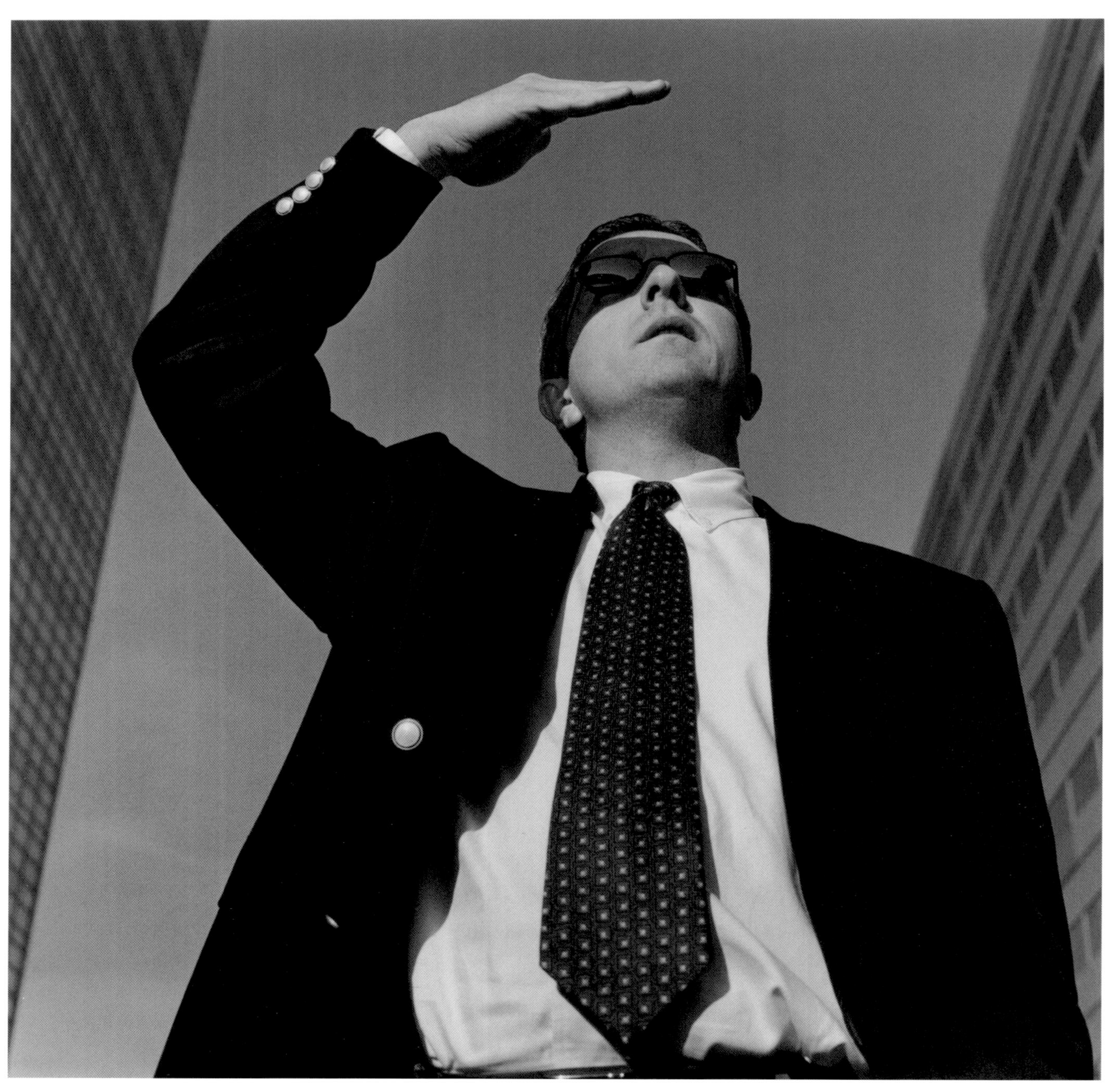

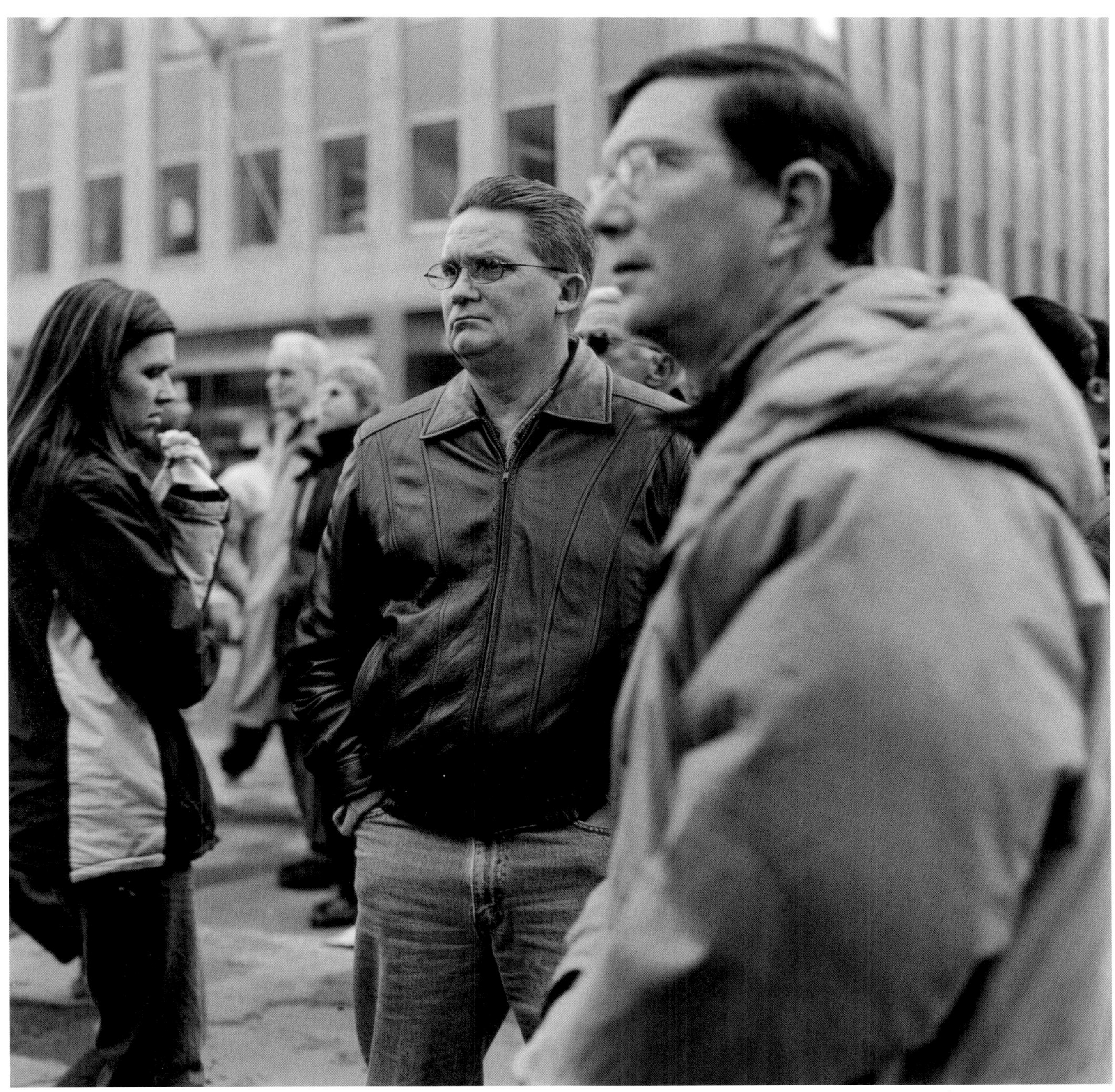

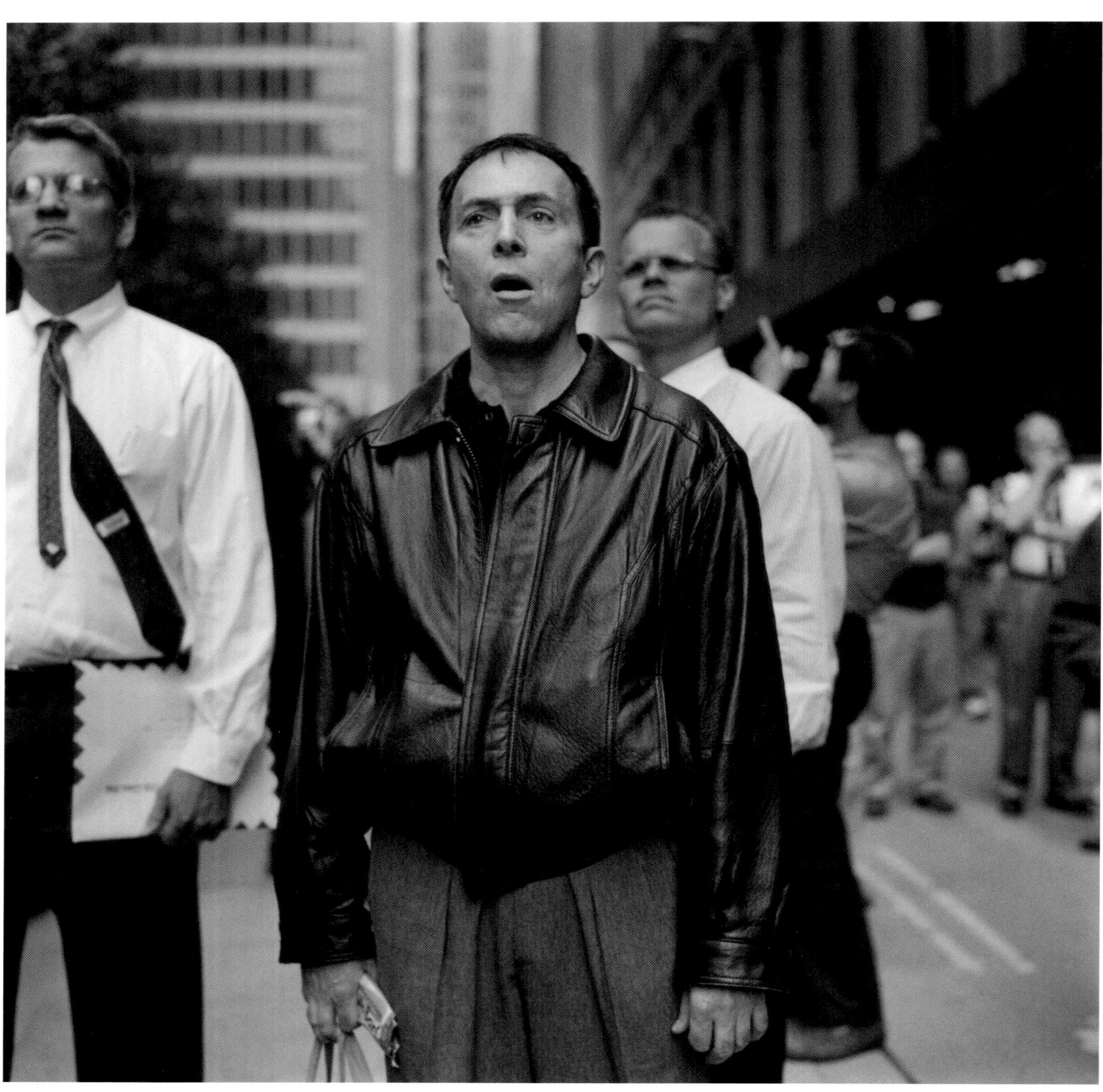

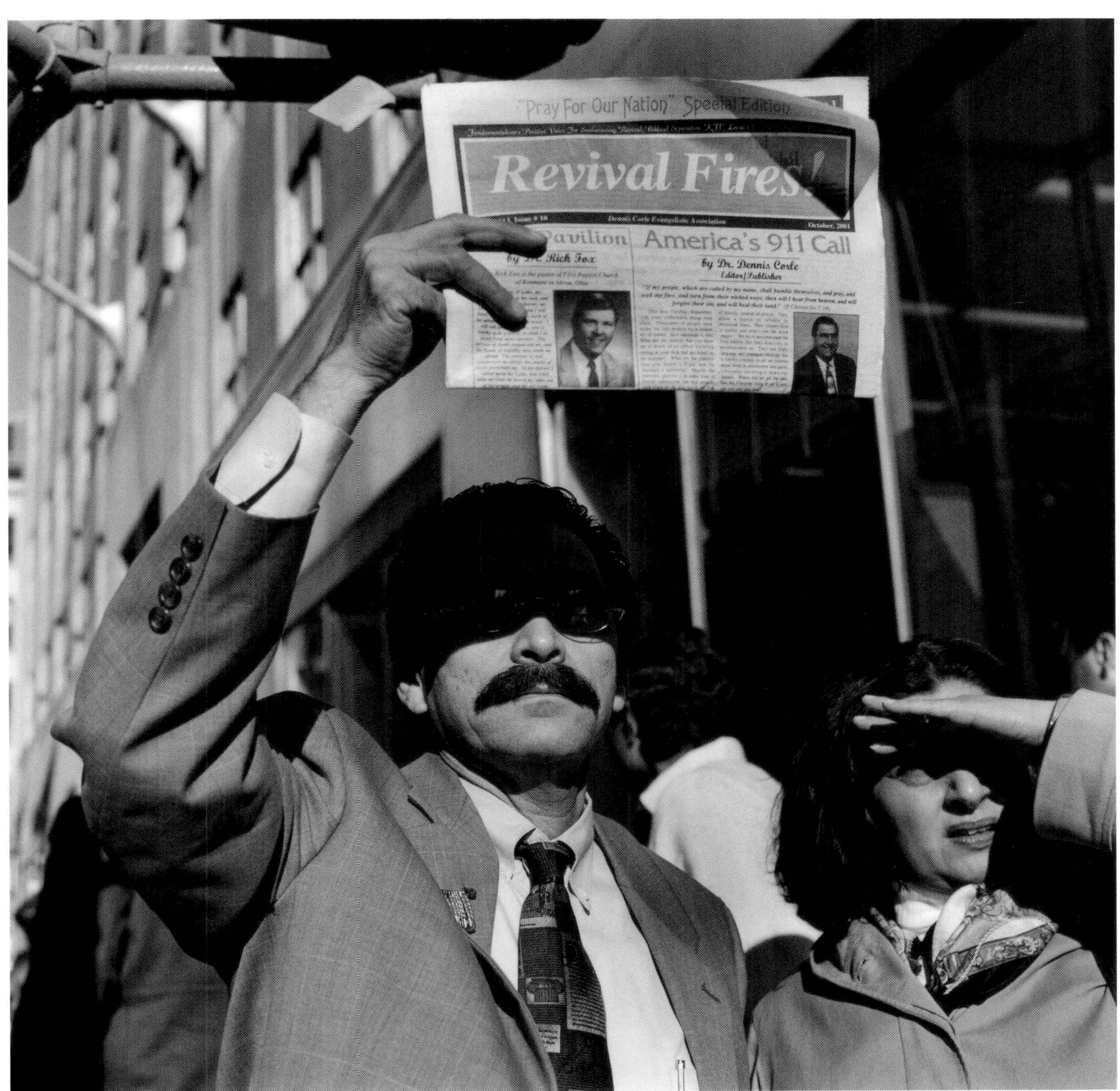
"Pray For Our Nation" Special Edition
Revival Fires!
America's 911 Call
by Dr. Dennis Corle
Editor/Publisher

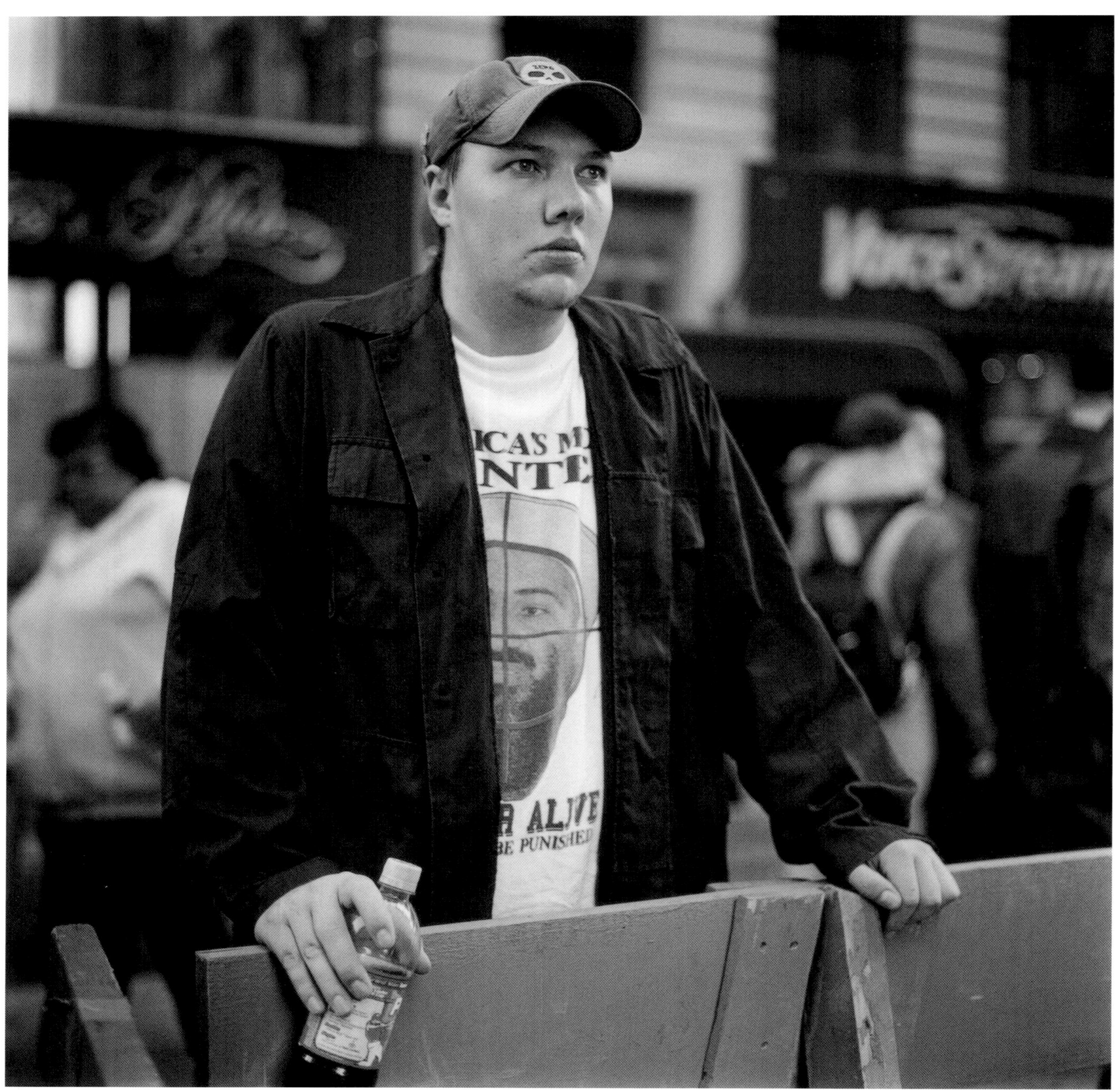
ICA'S M
NTE
R ALIVE
BE PUNISHED

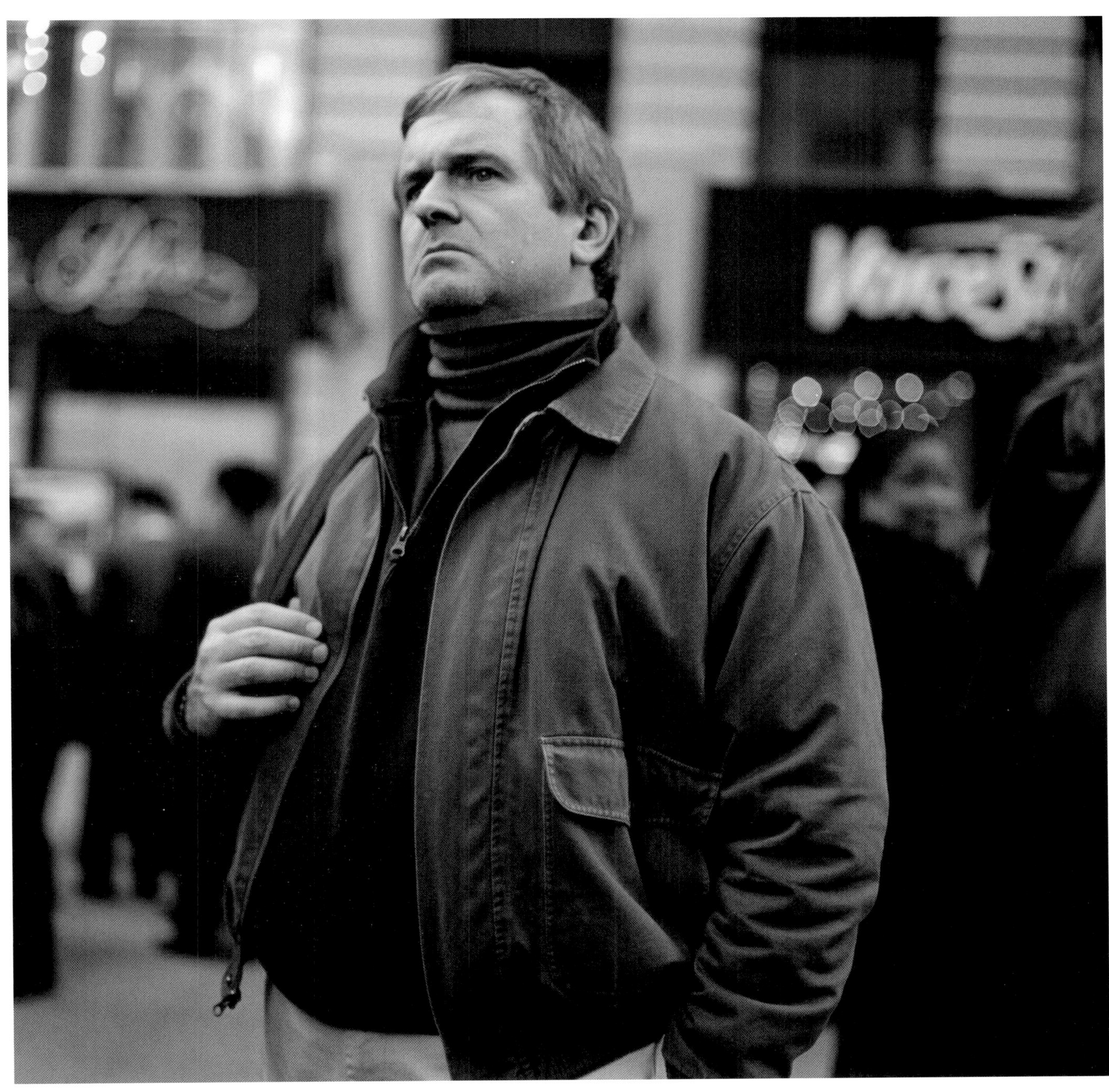

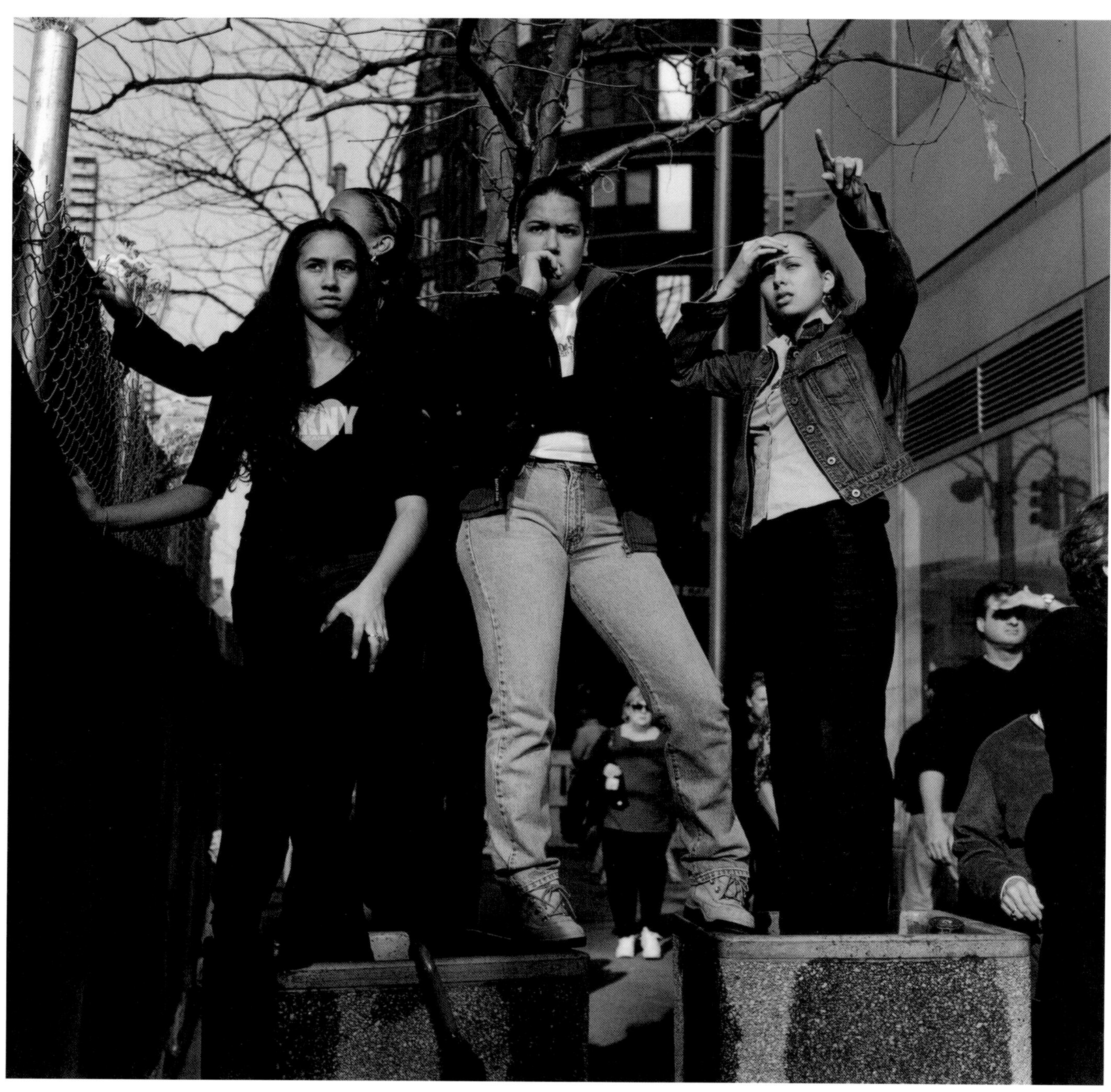

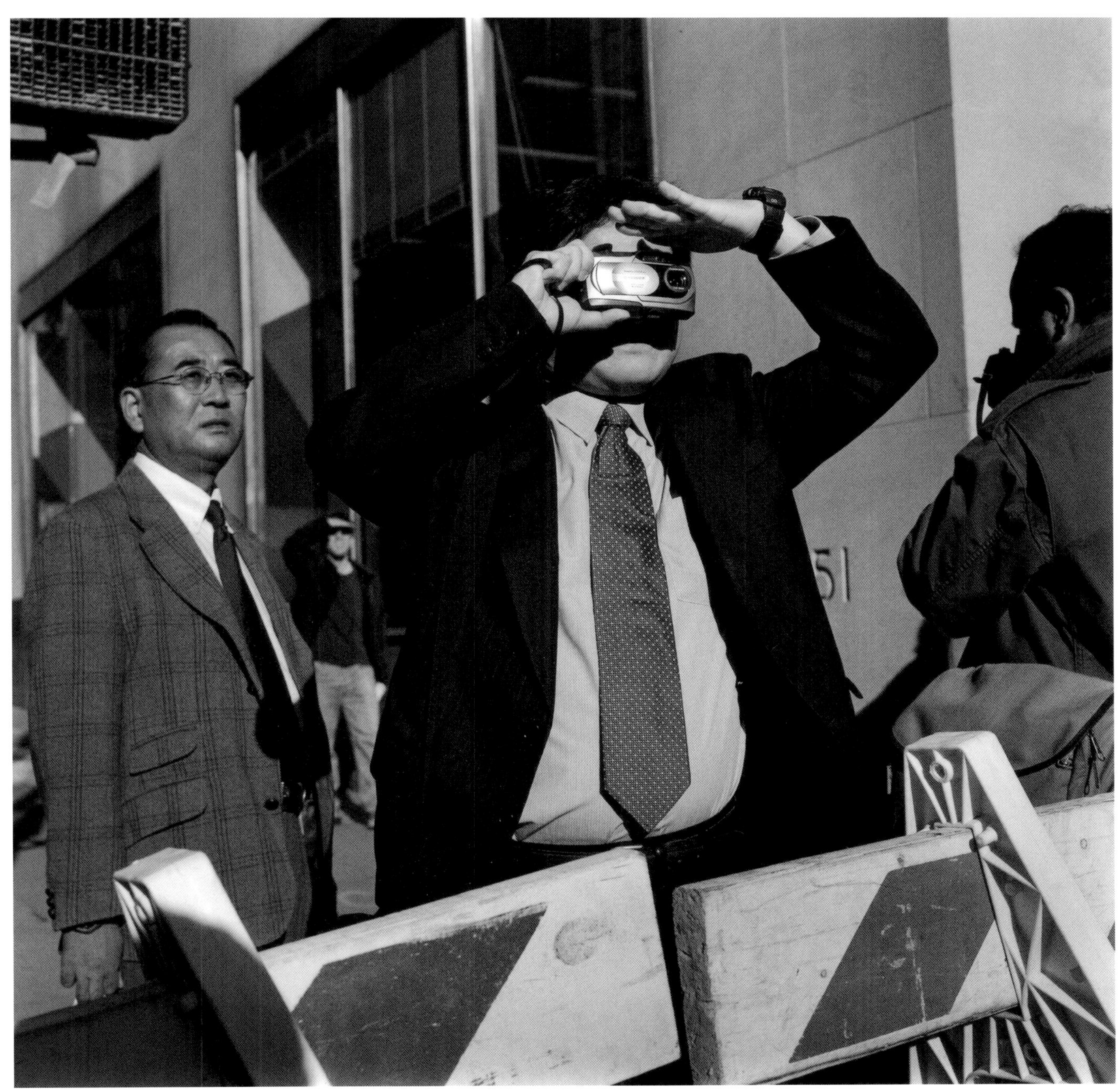
51

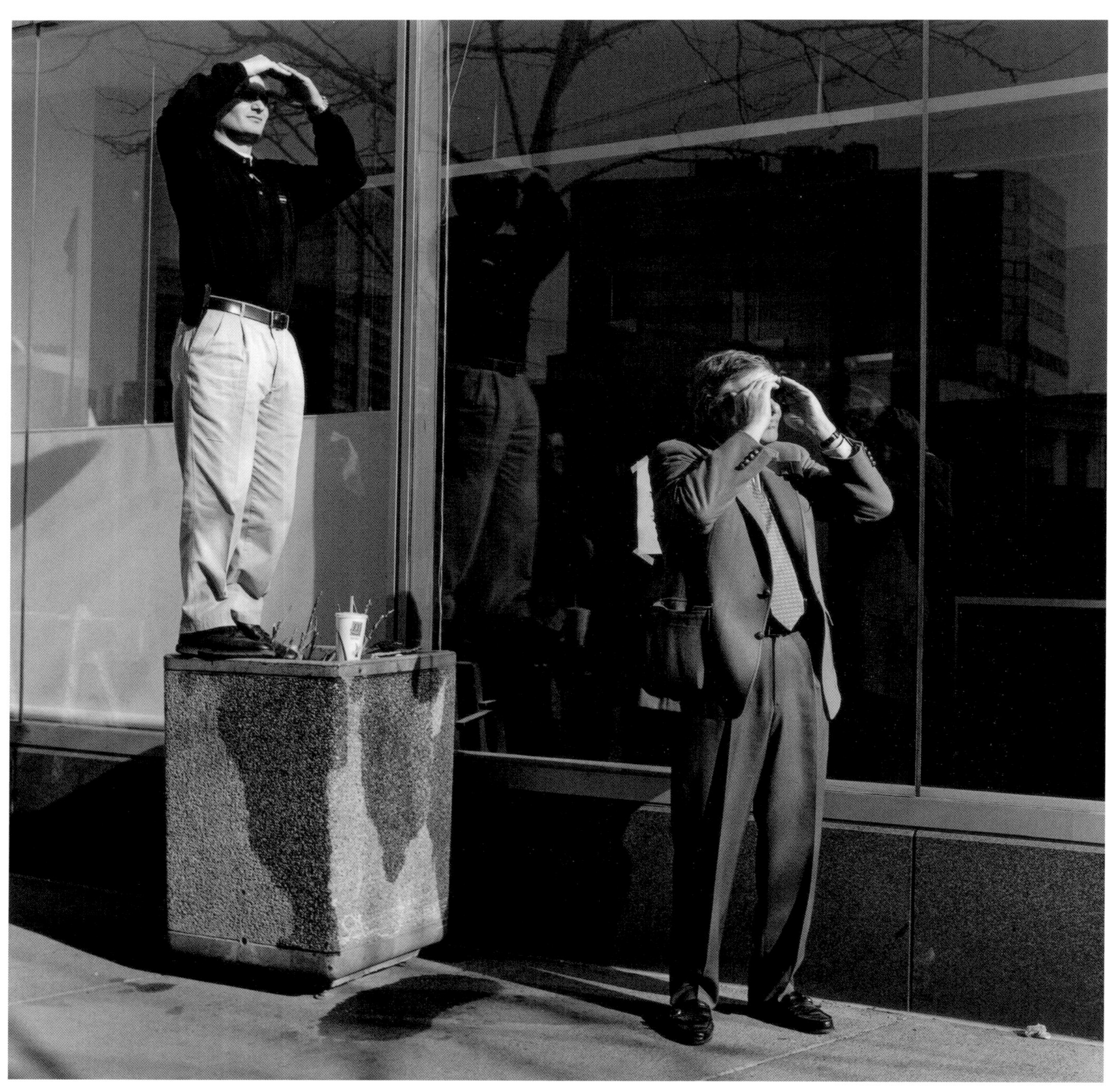

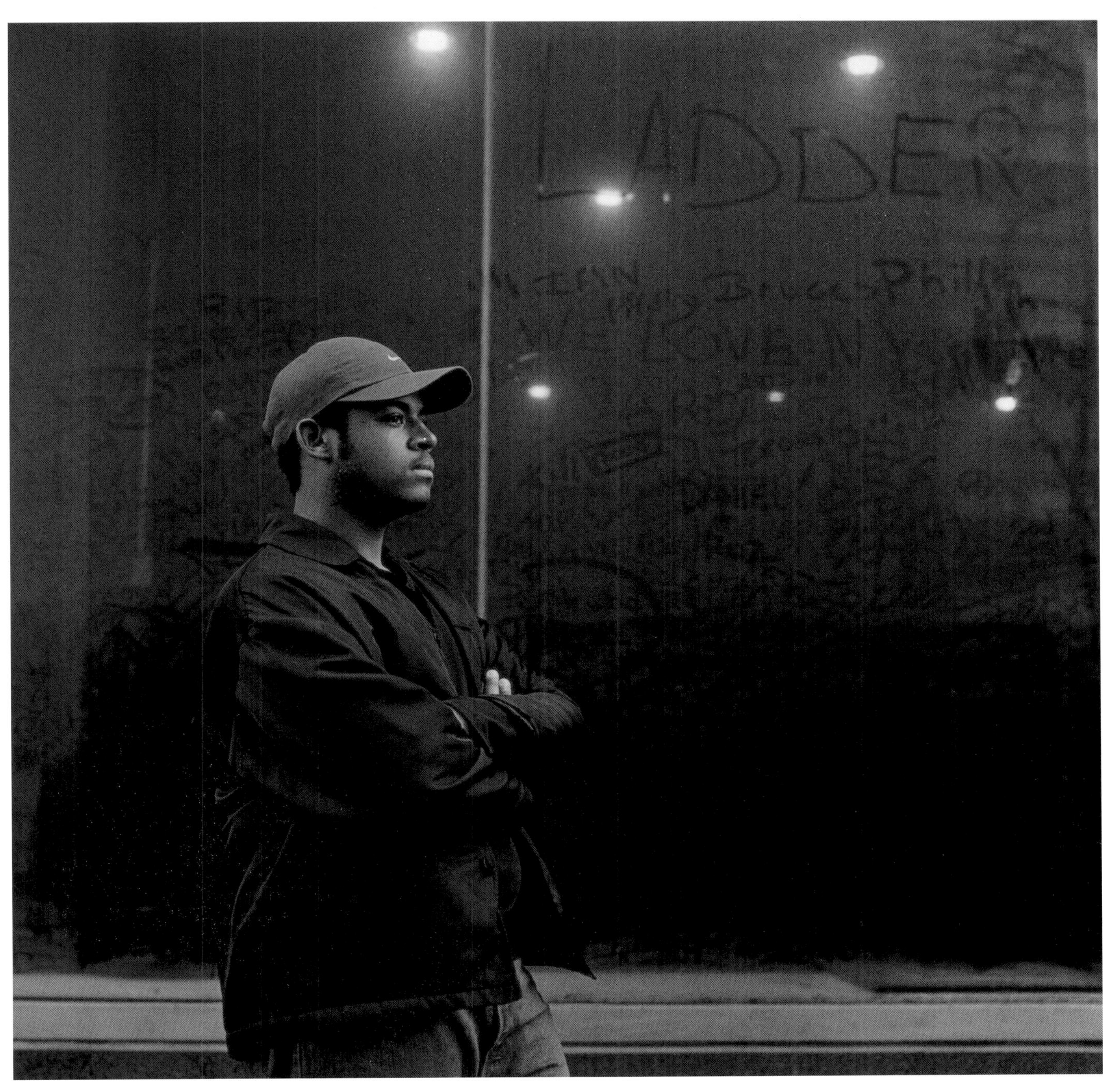
LADDER

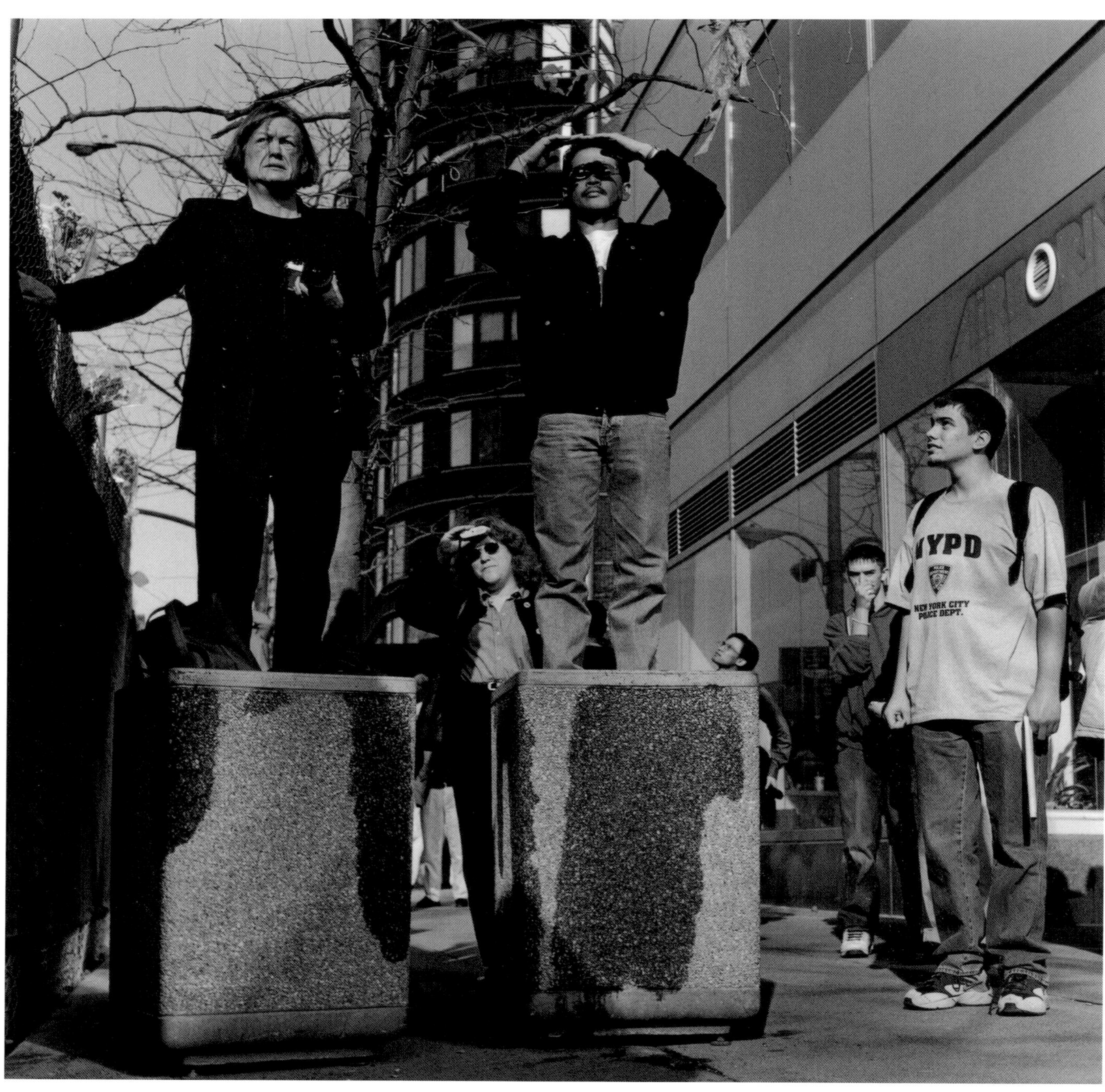
NYPD
NEW YORK CITY
POLICE DEPT.

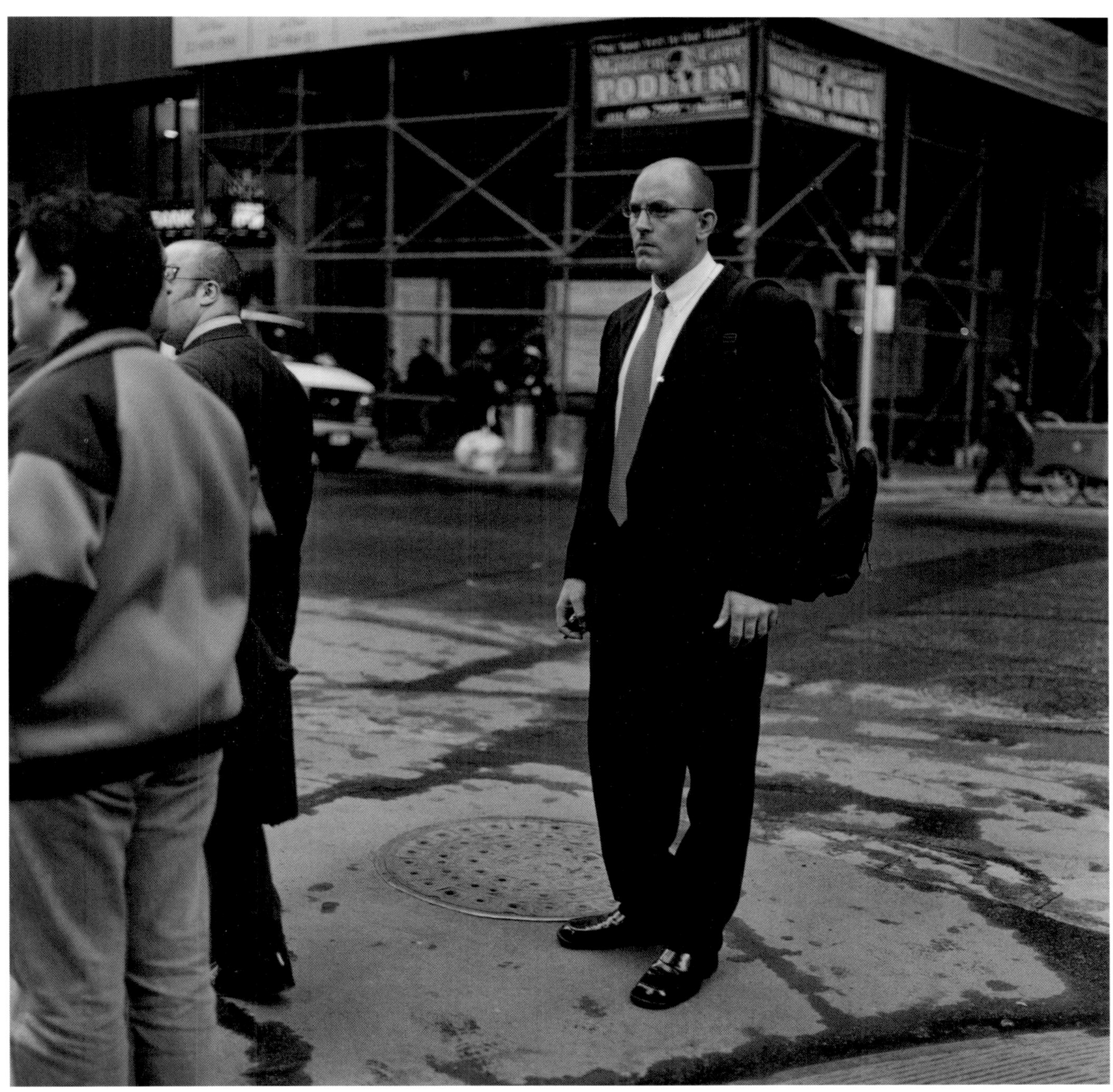
PODIATRY

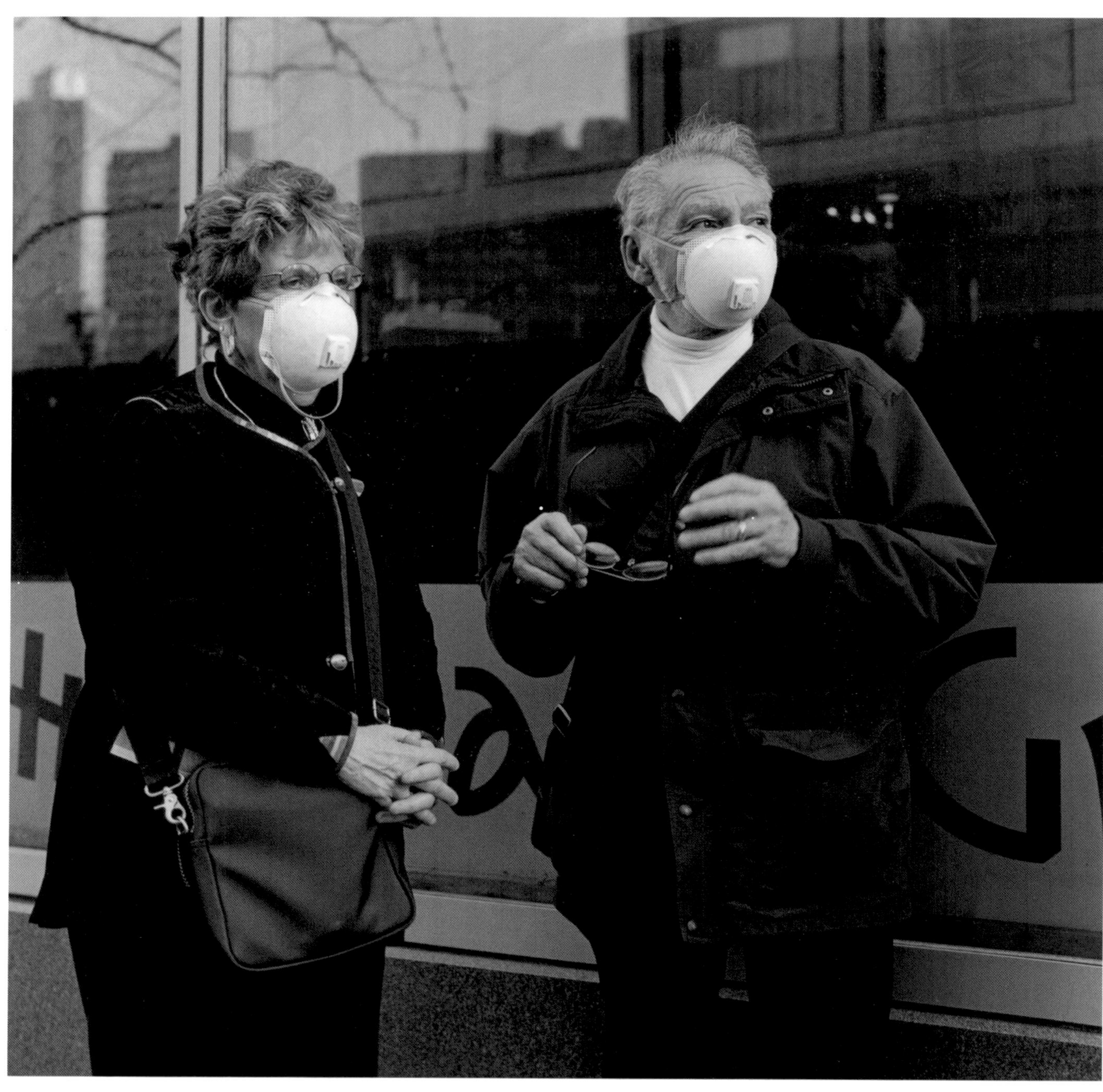

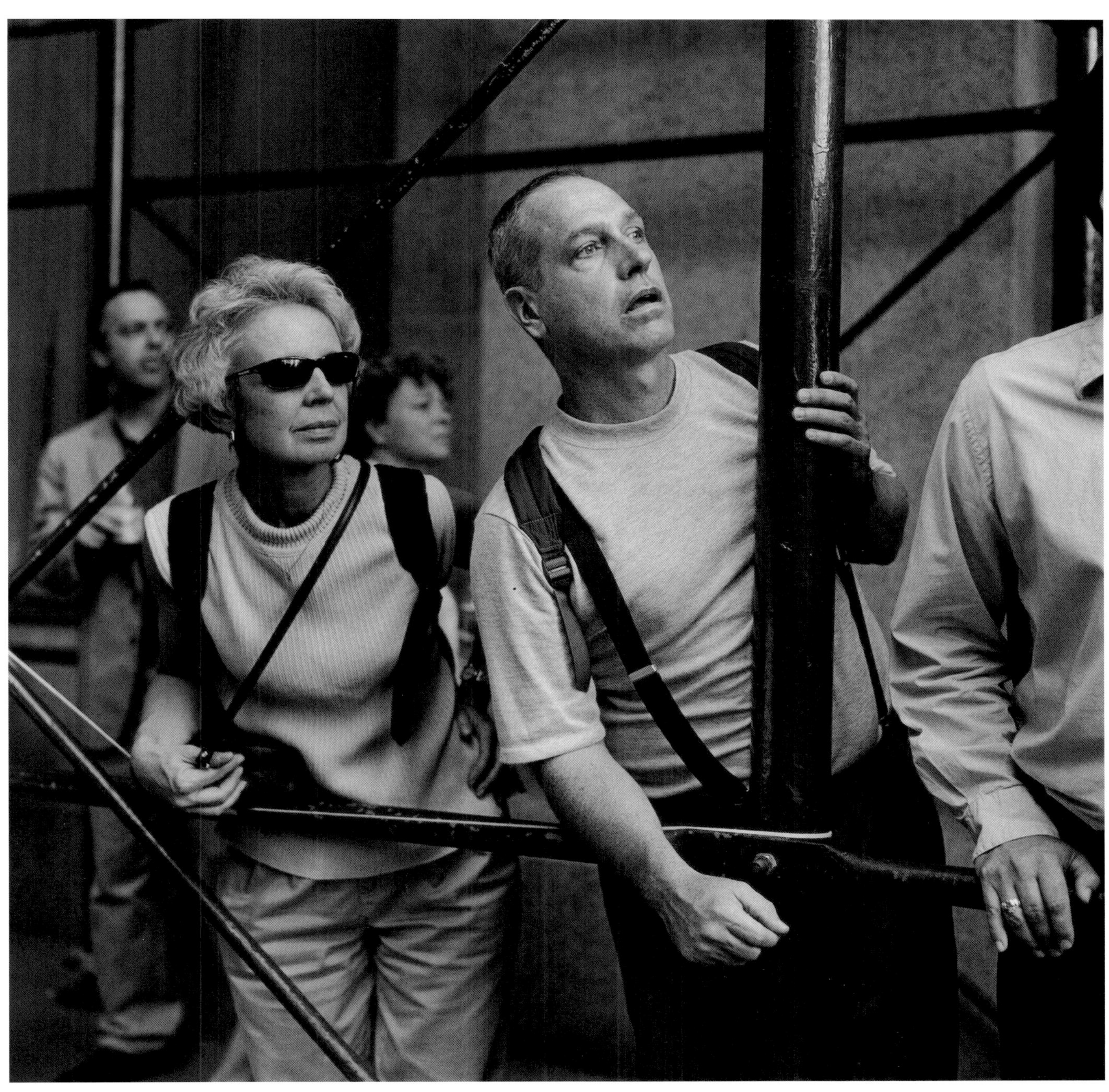

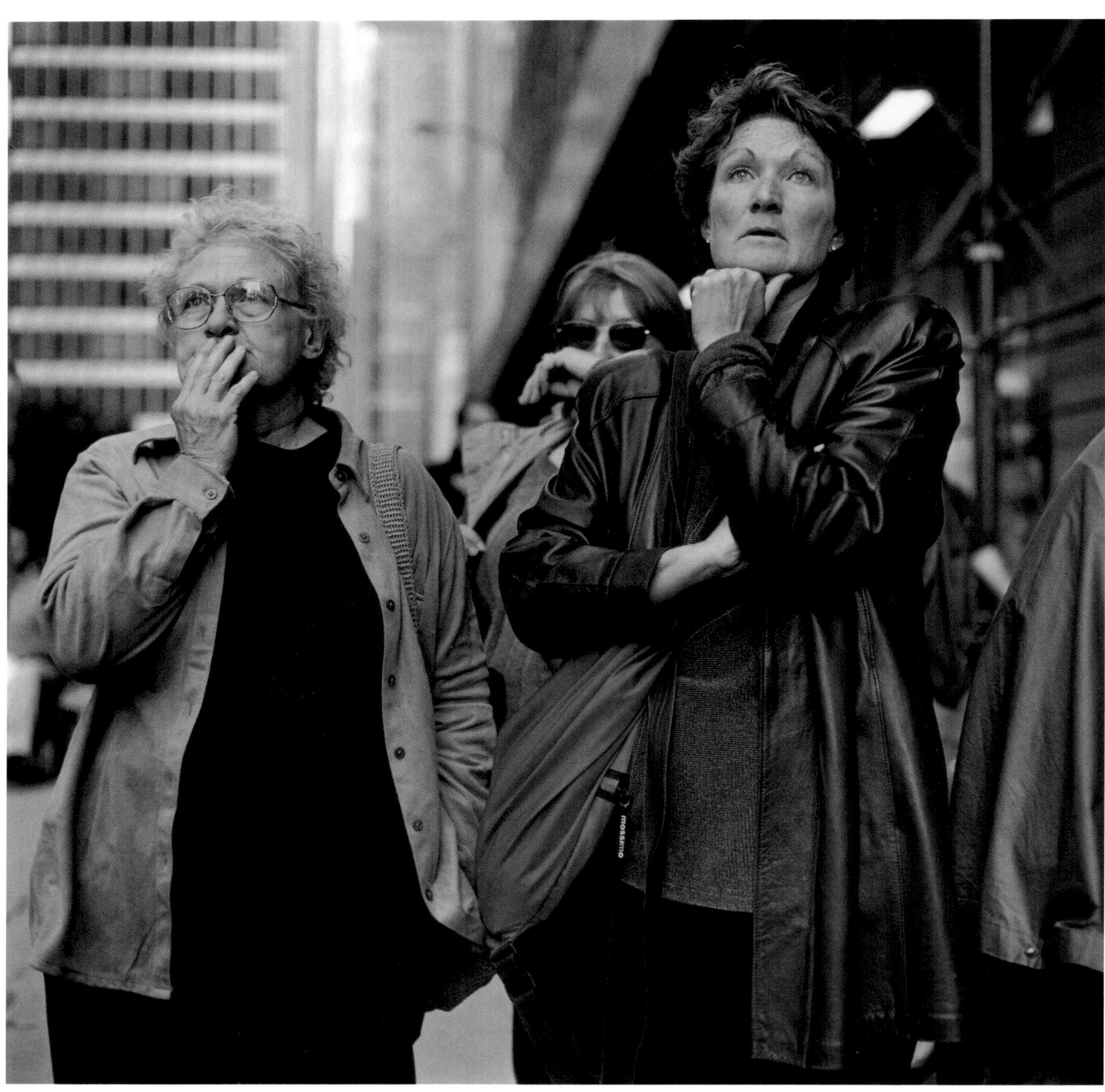
mossimo

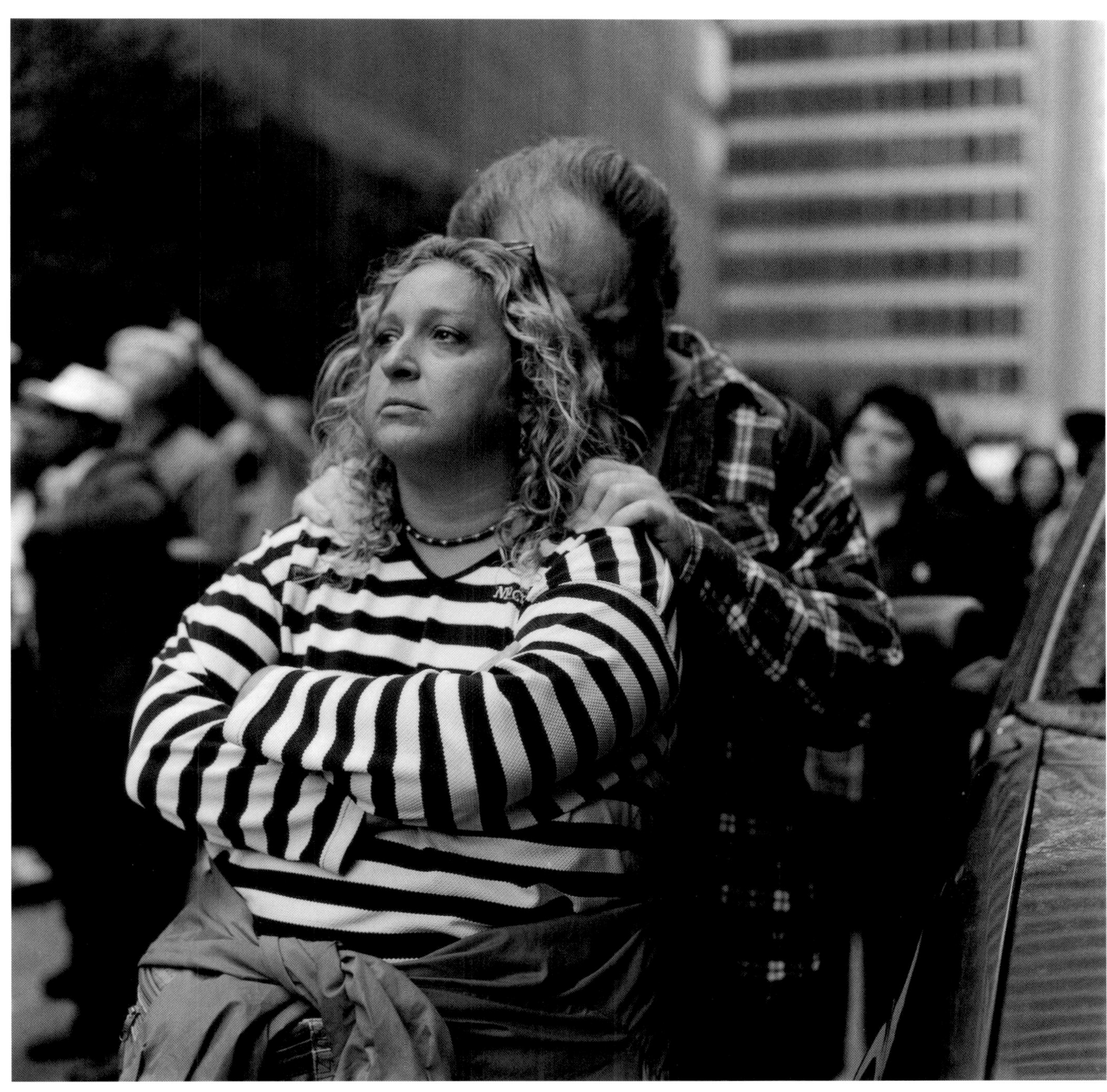

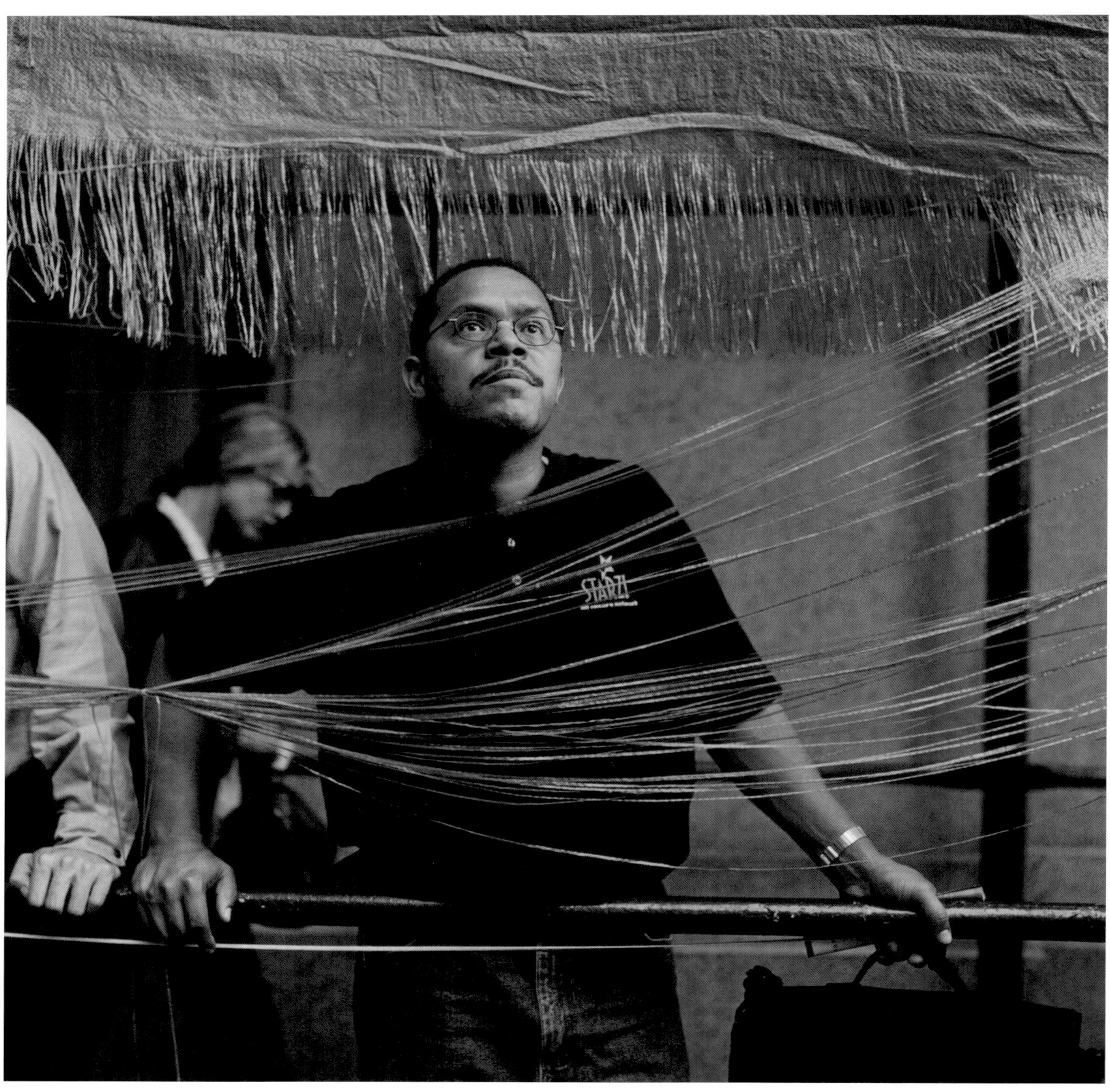

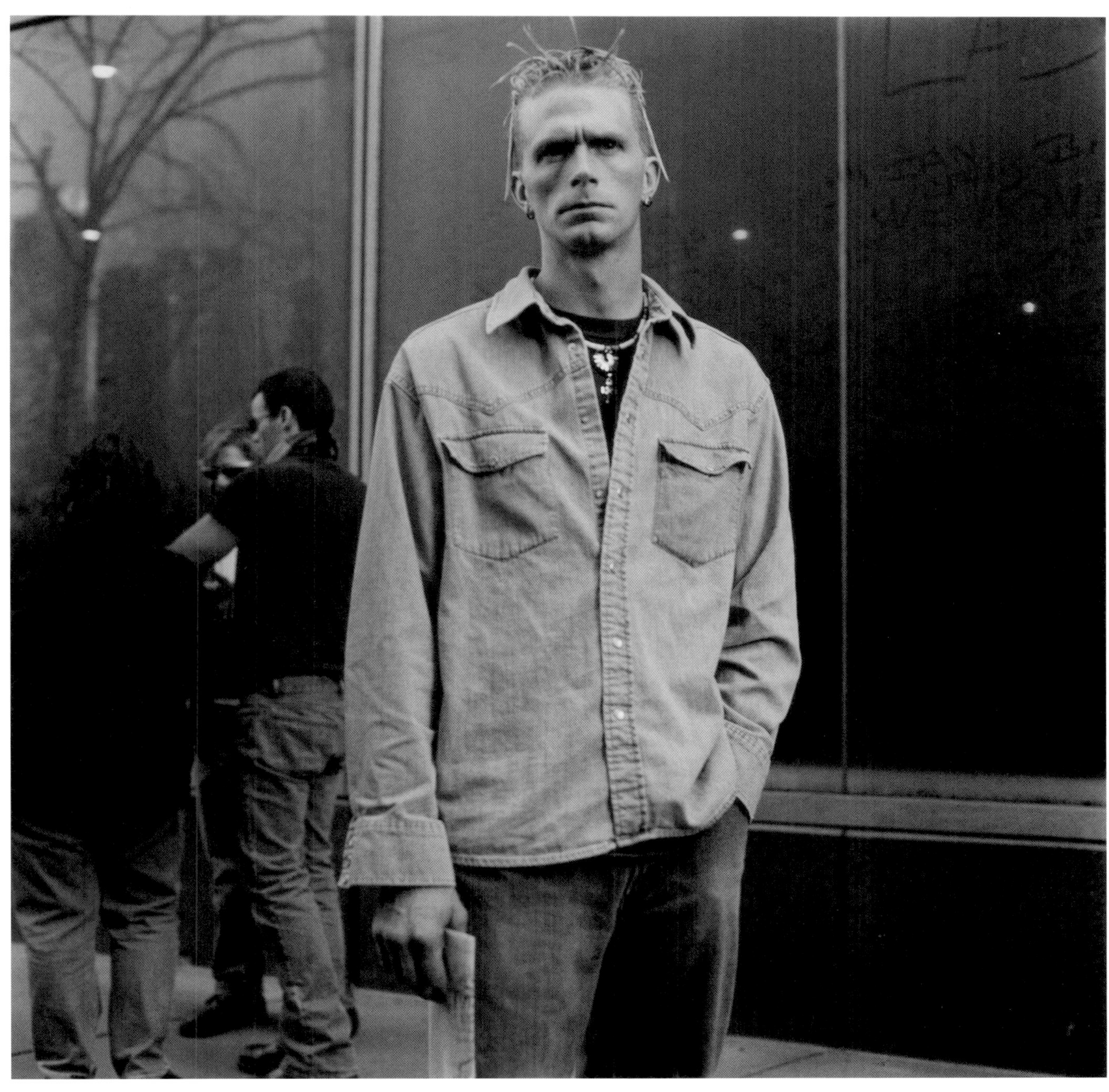

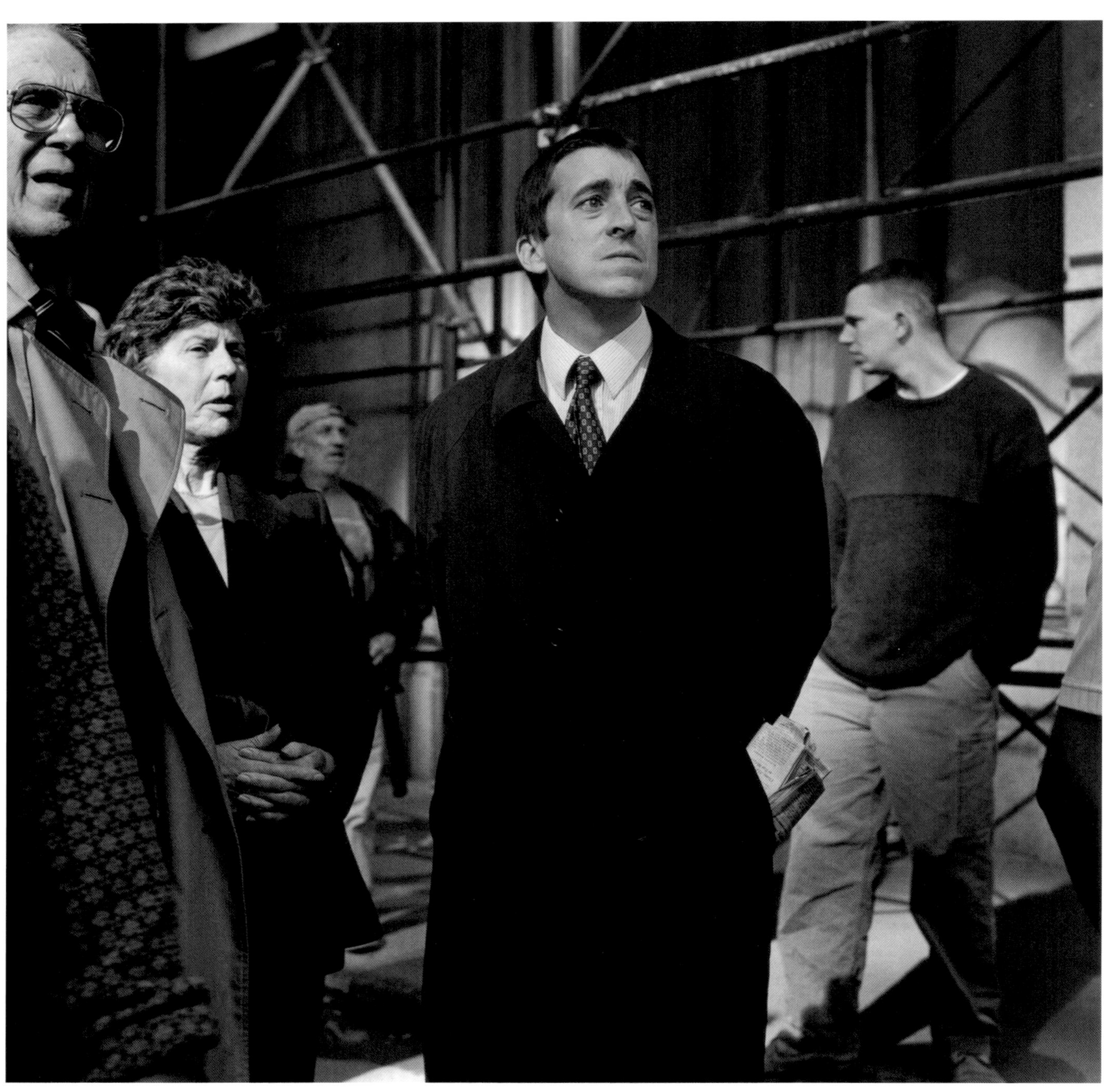

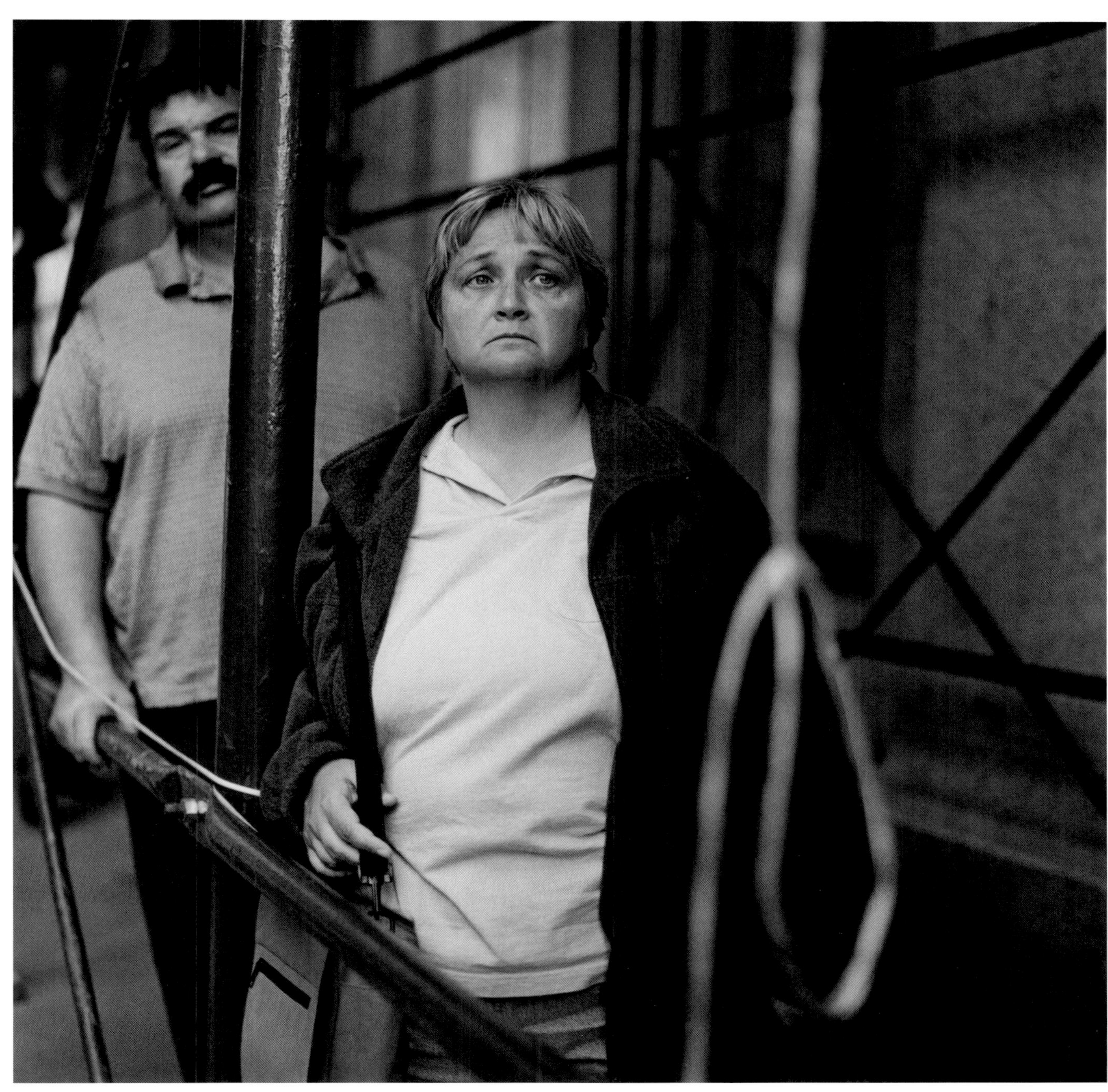

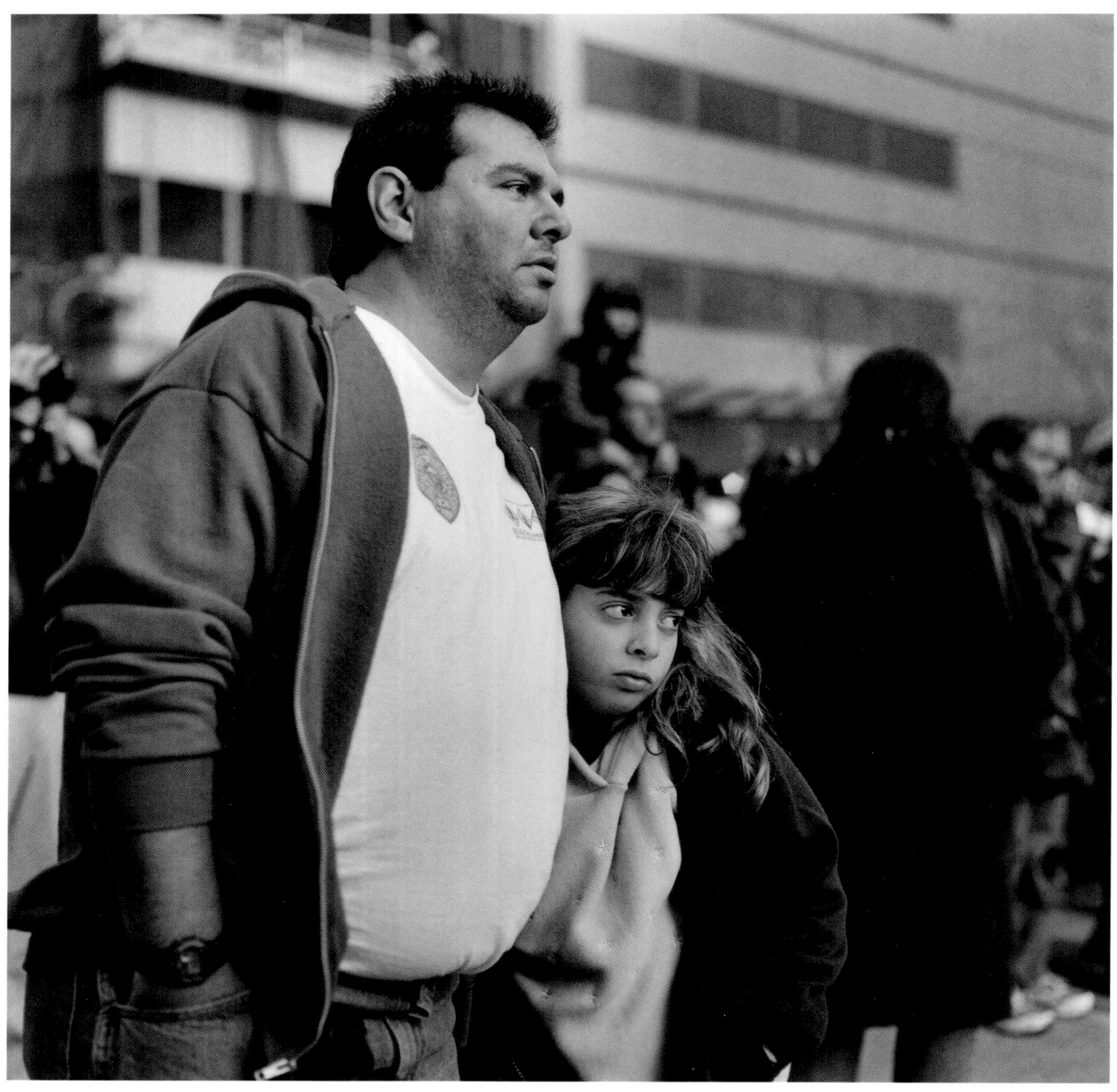

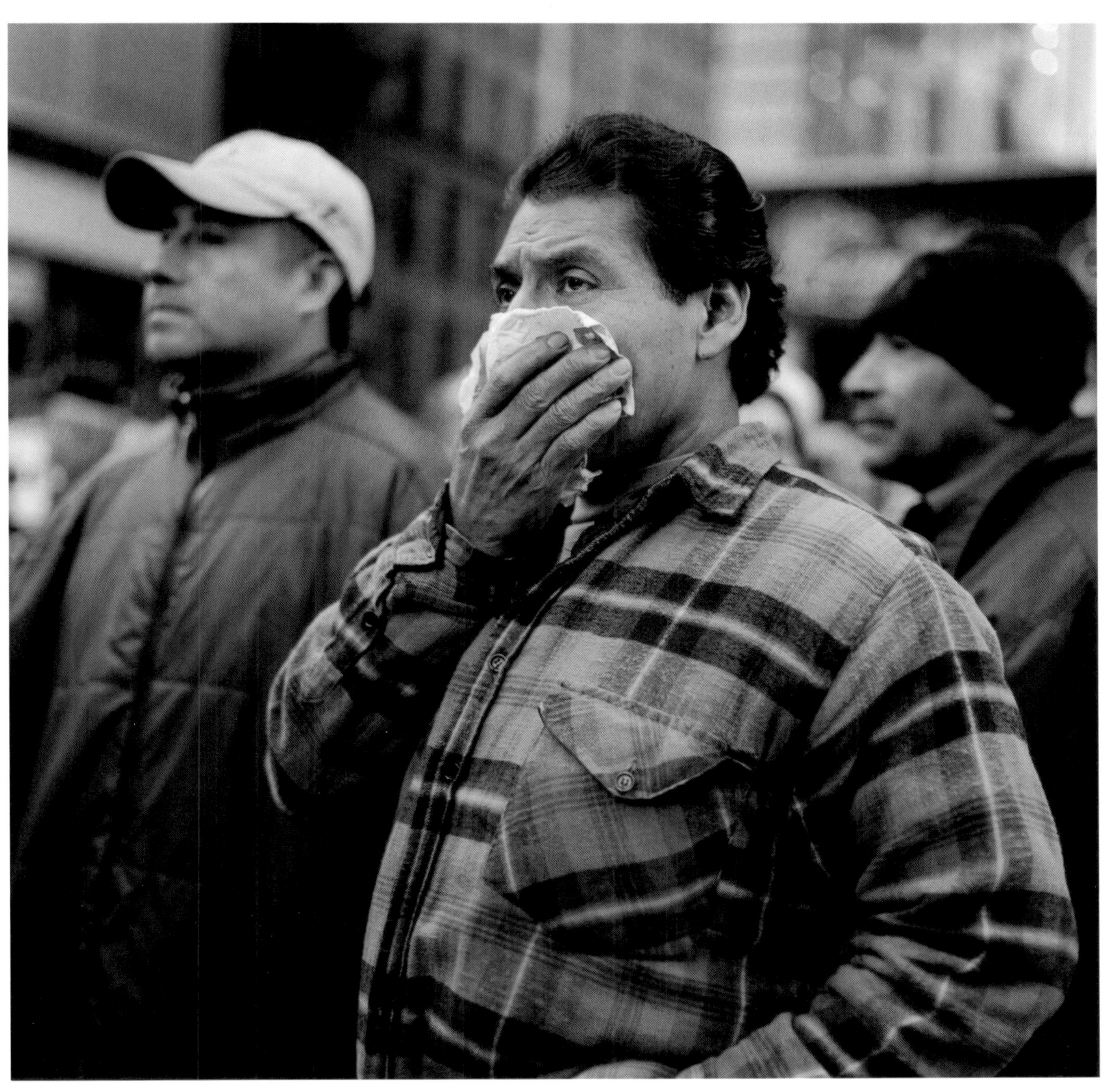

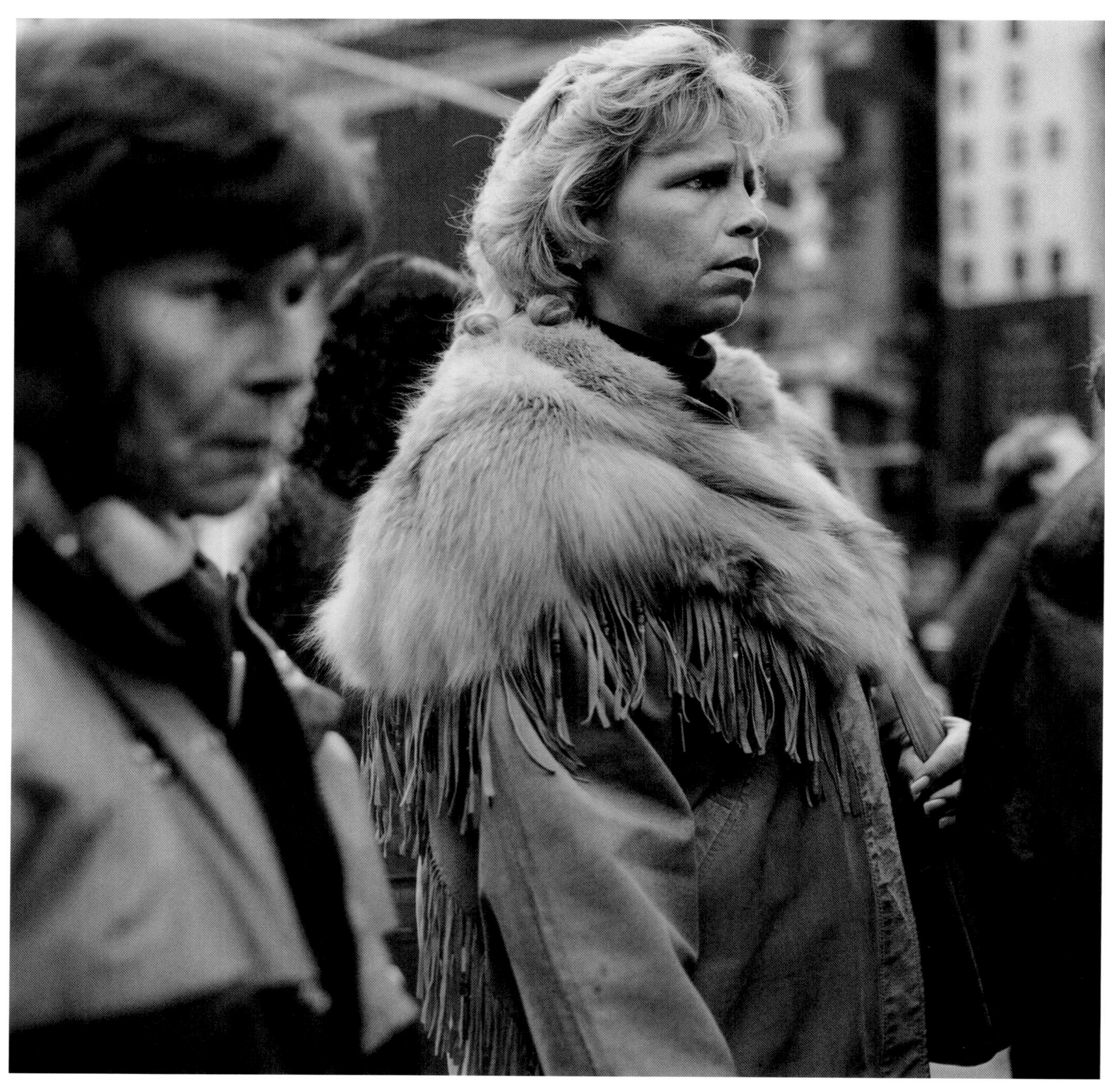

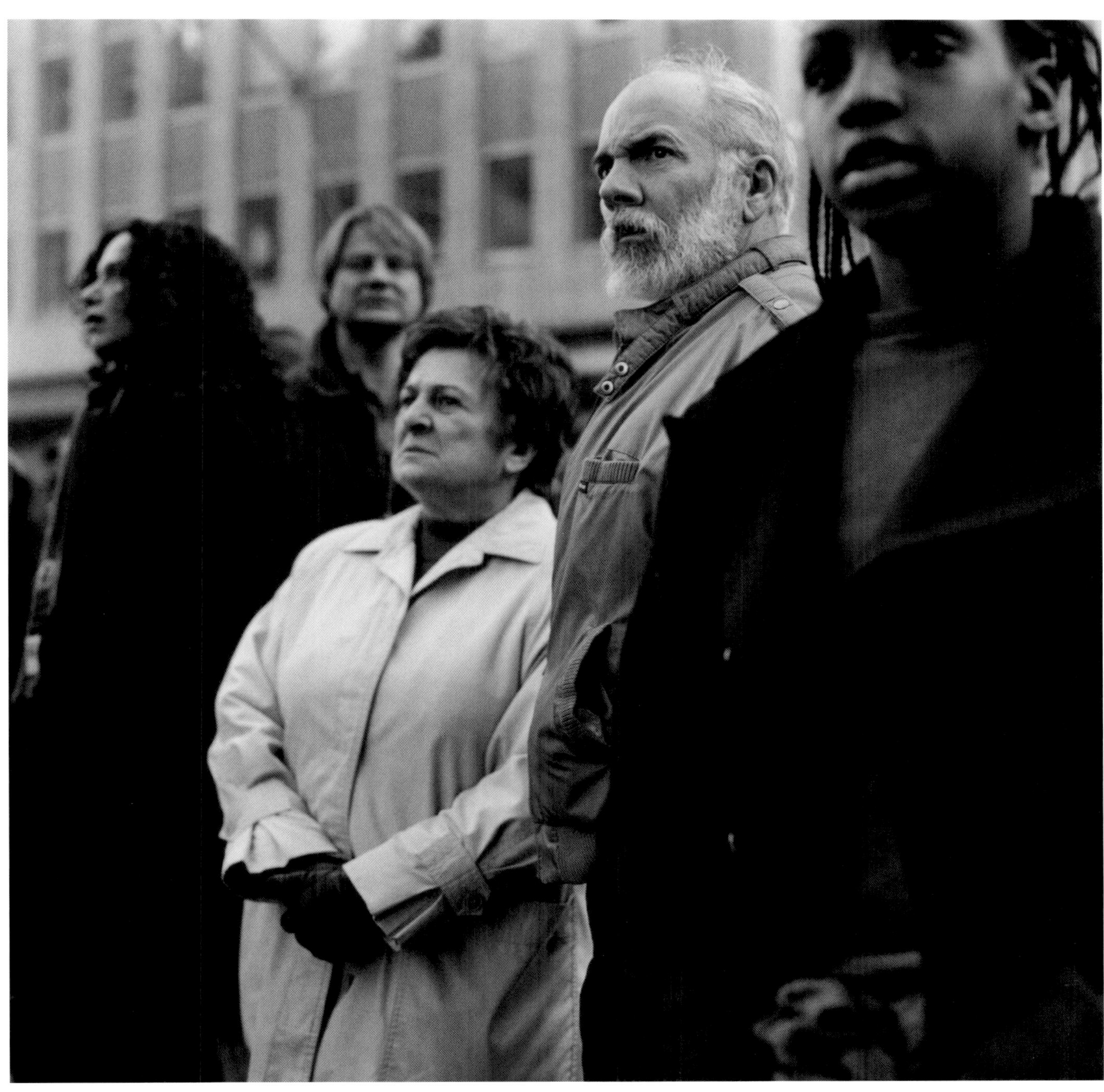

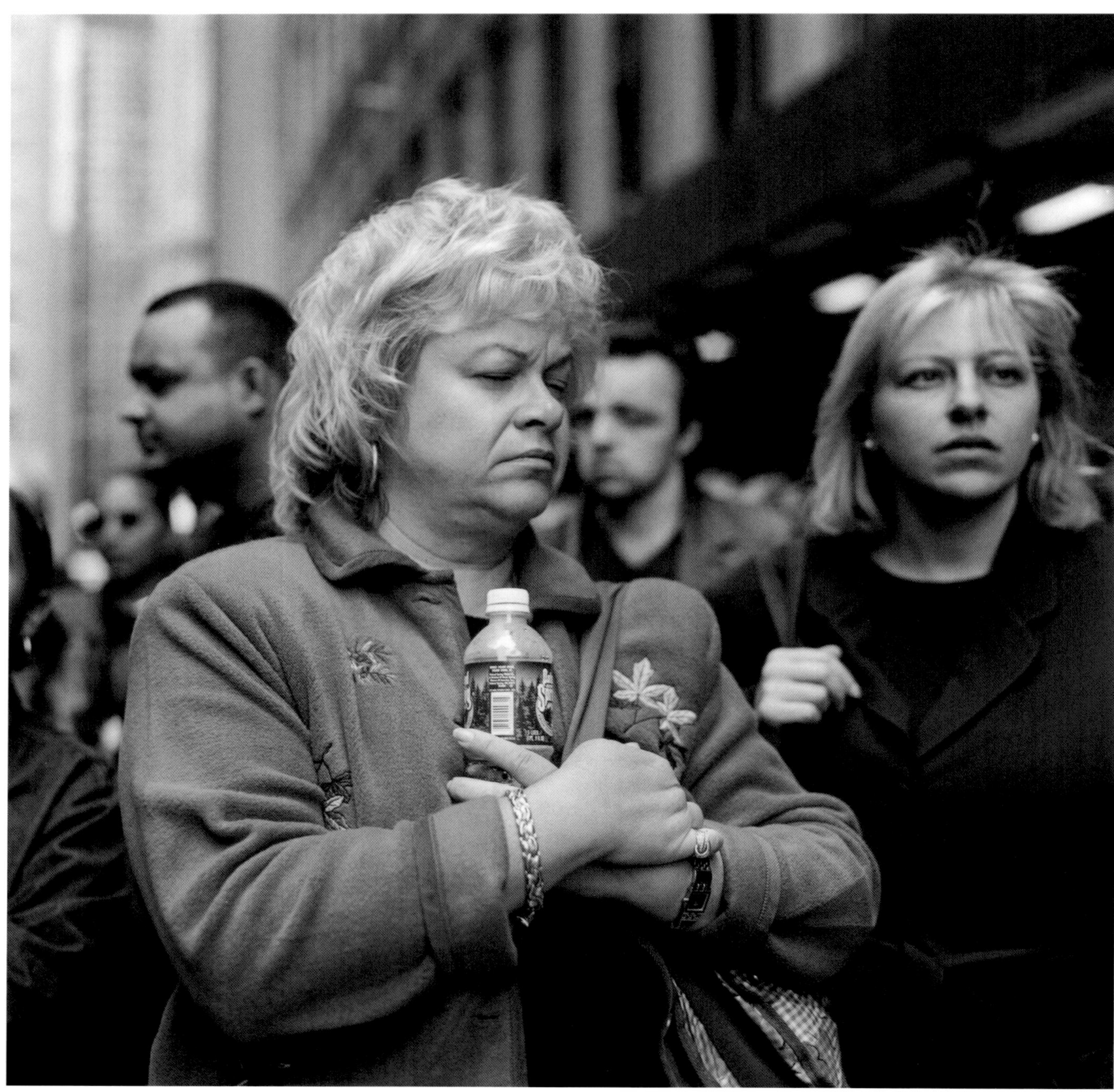

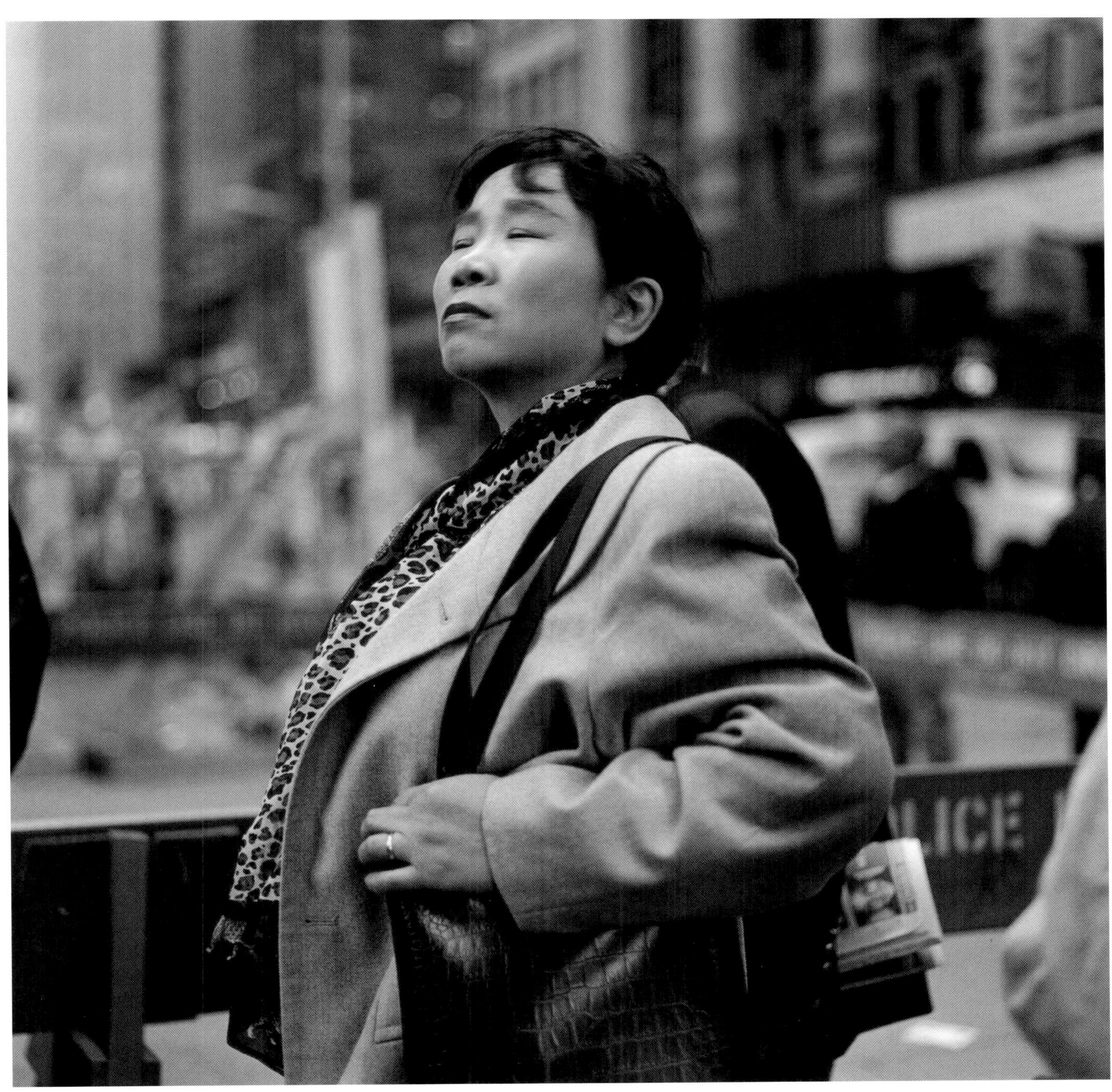
LICE

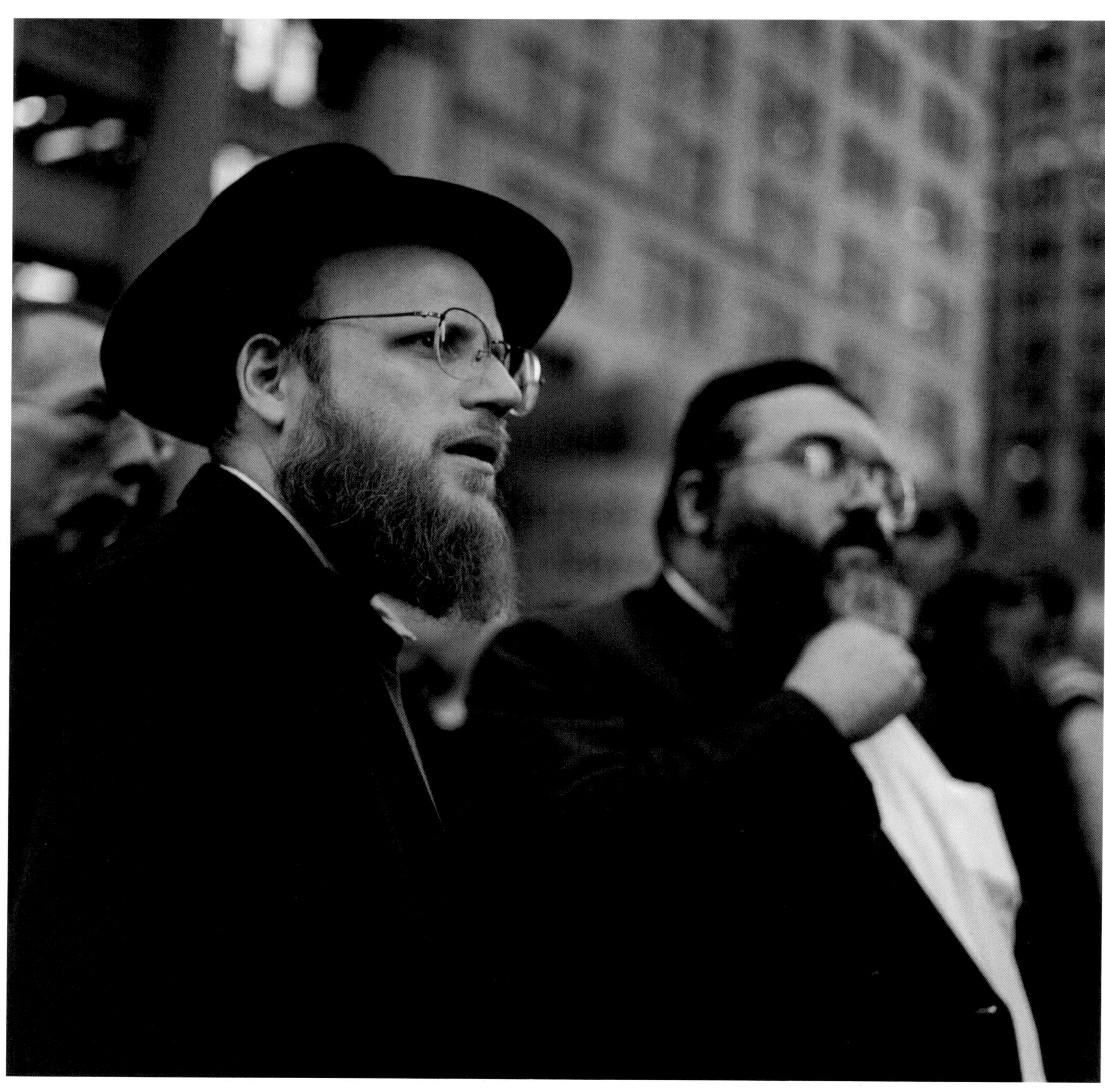

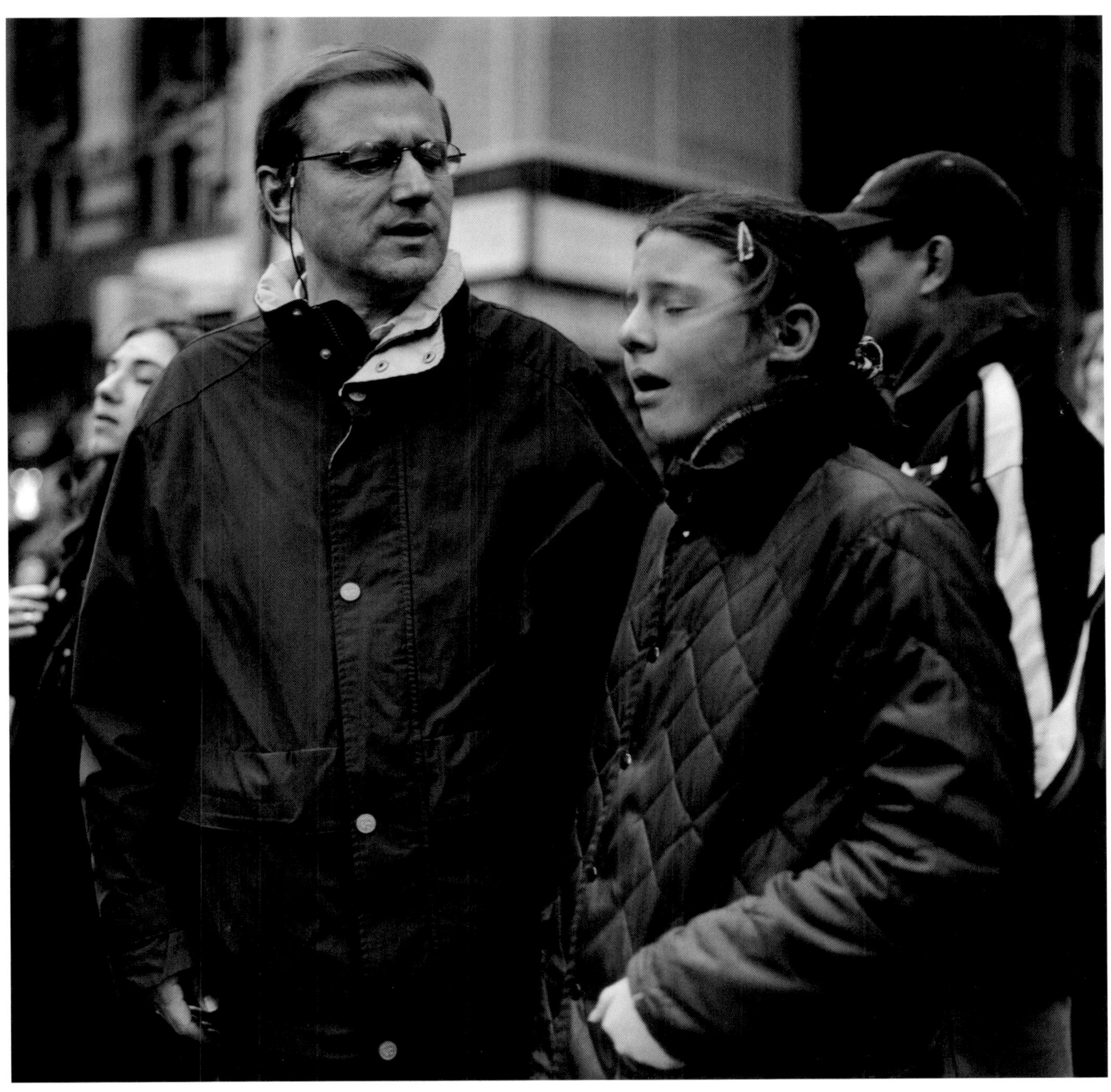

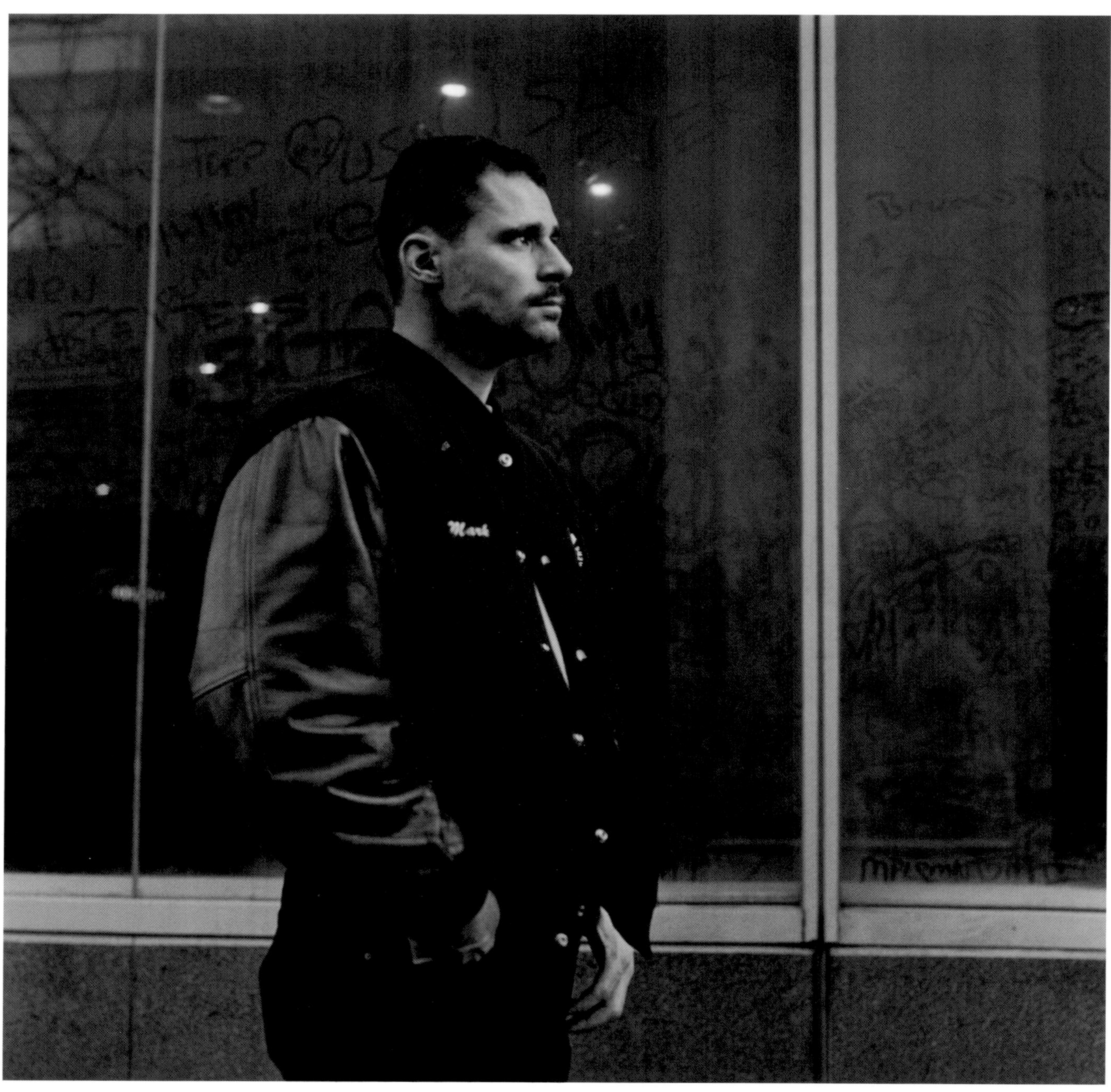

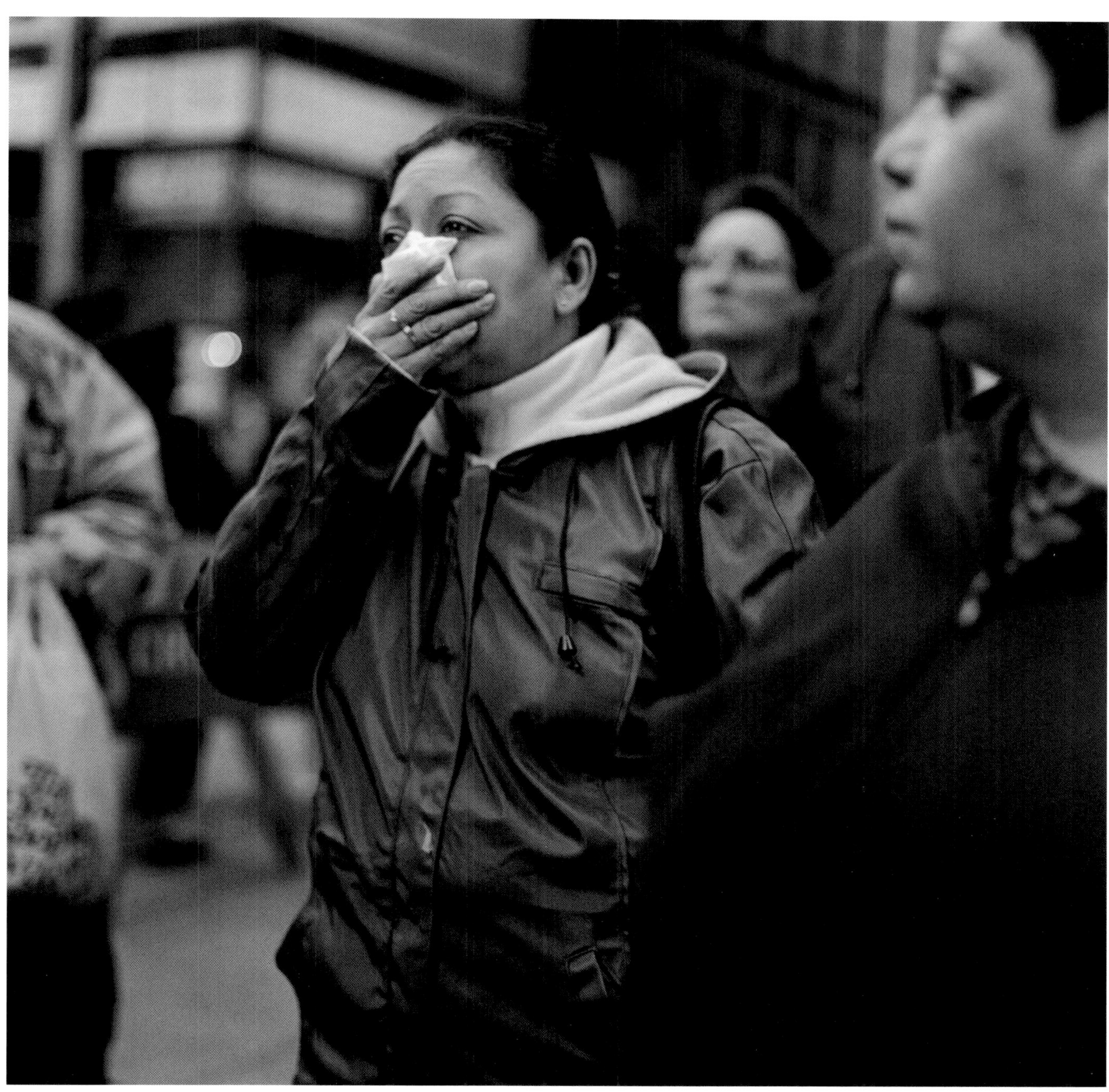

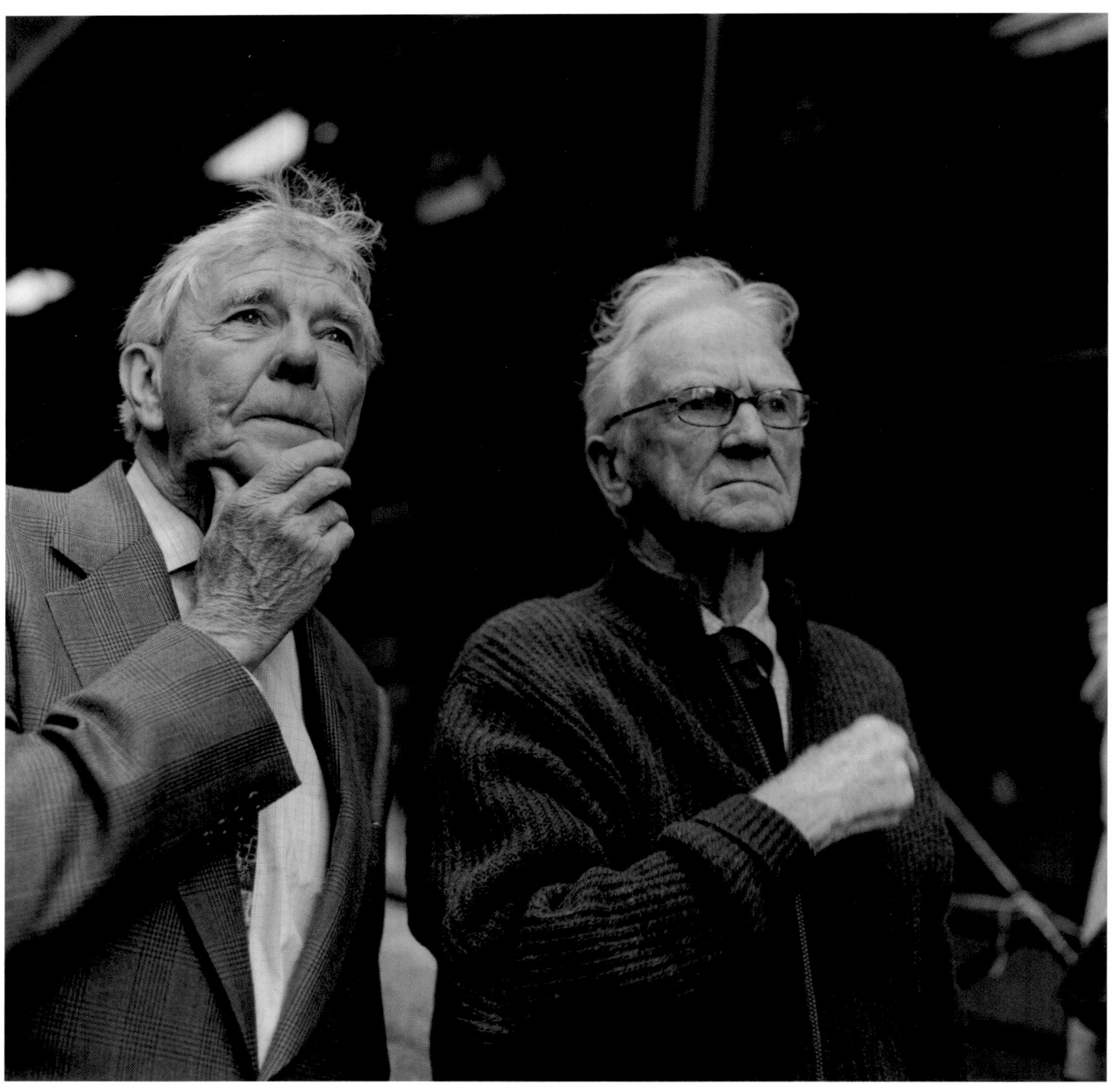

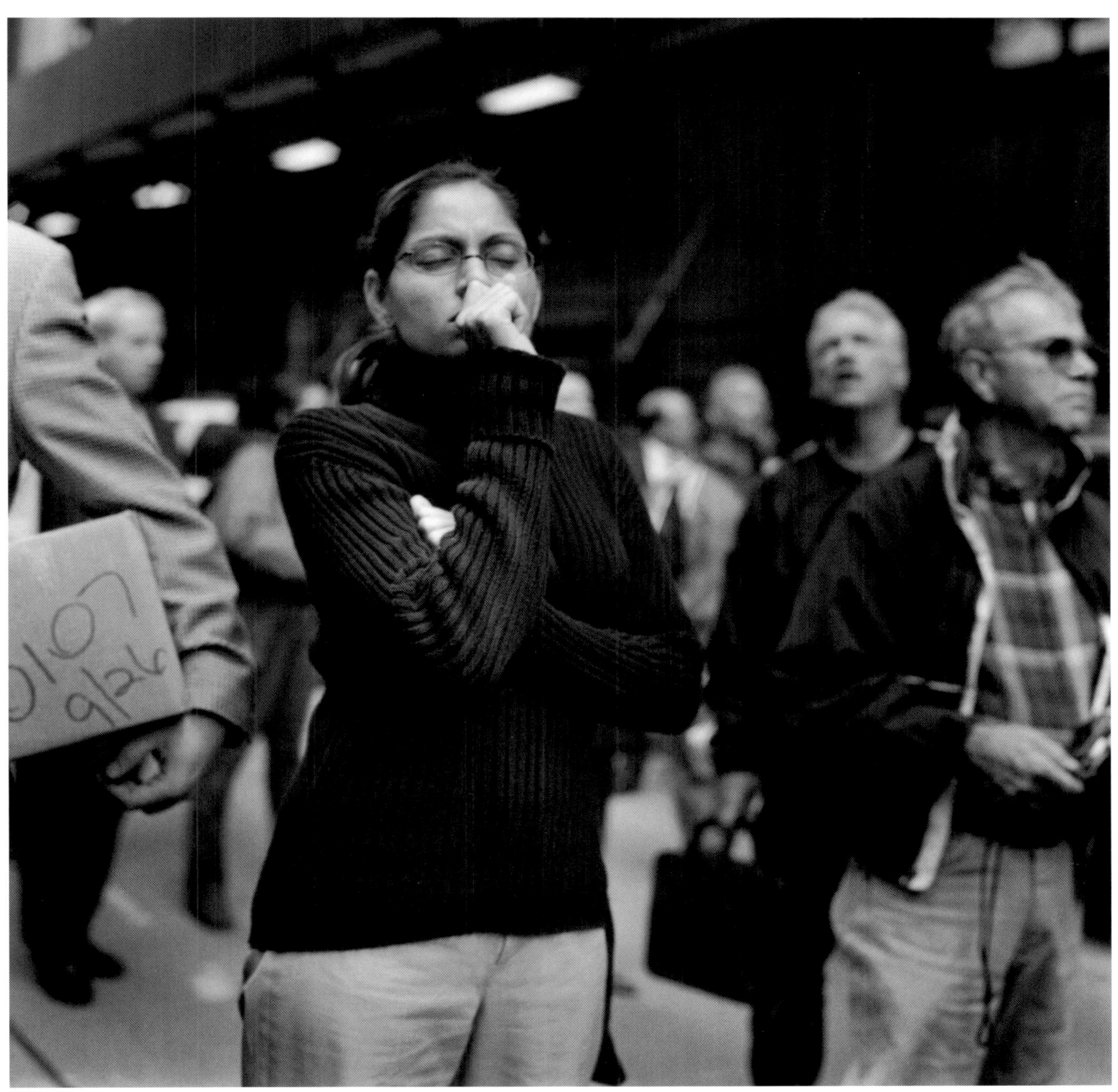

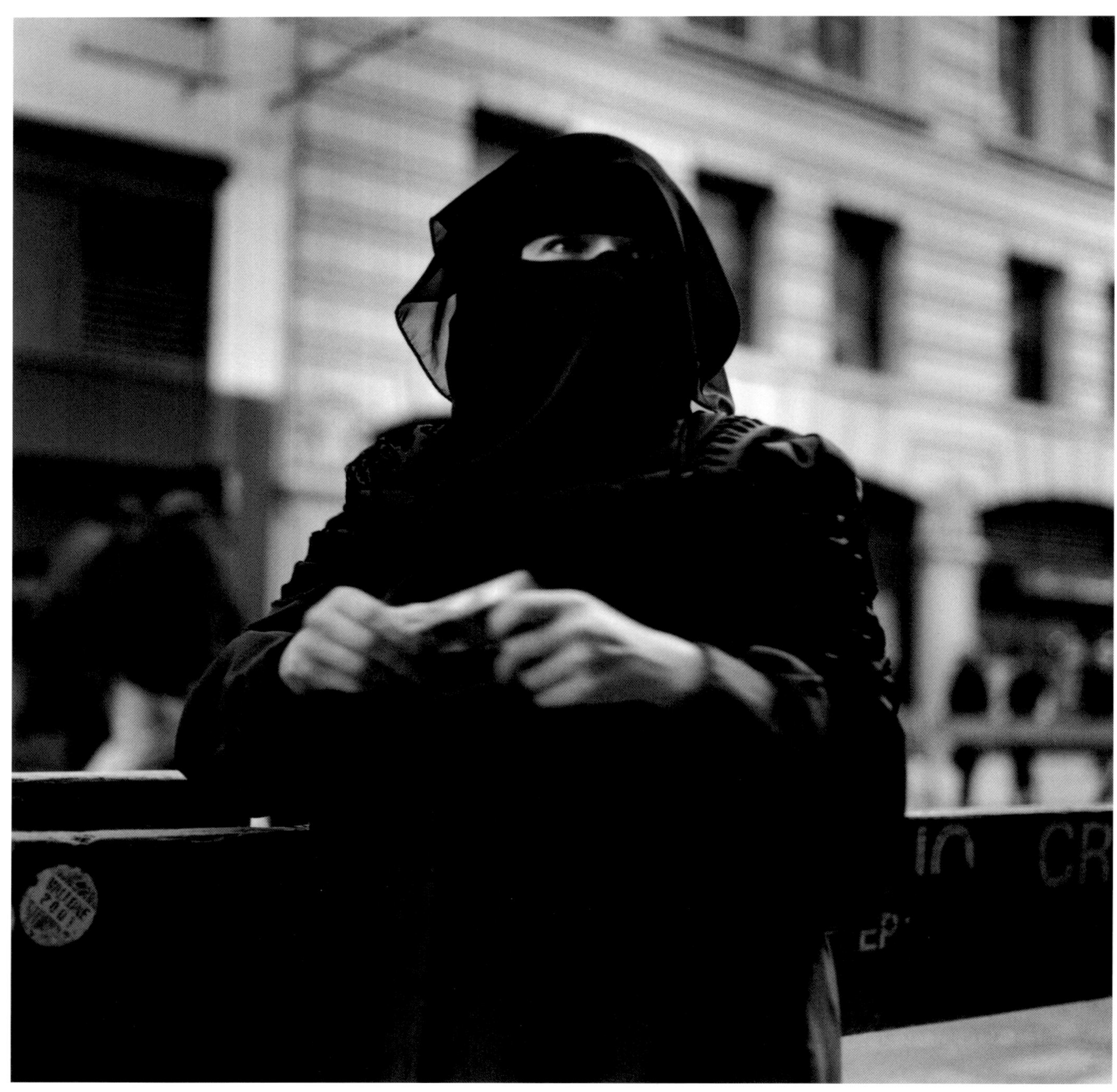

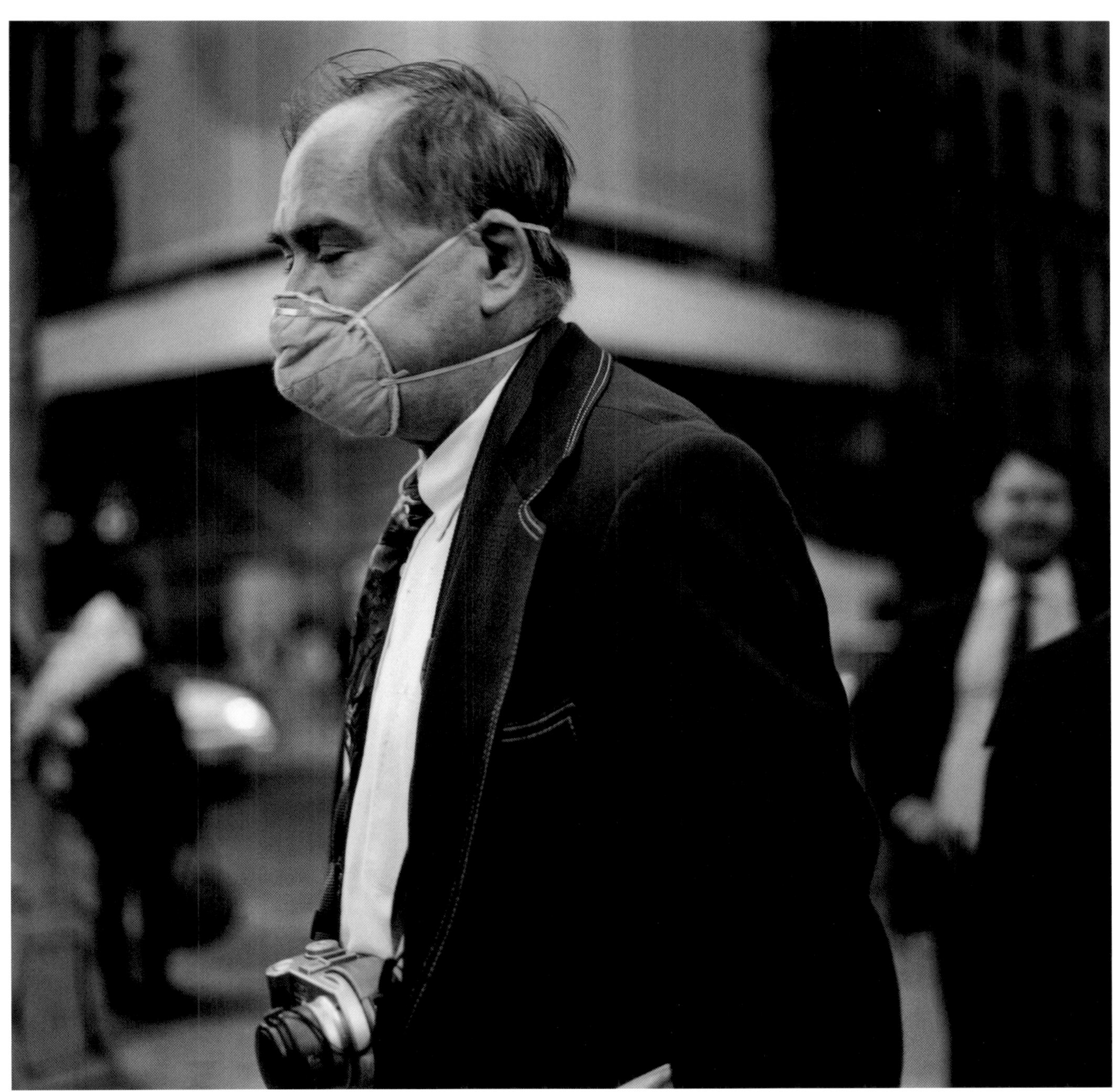

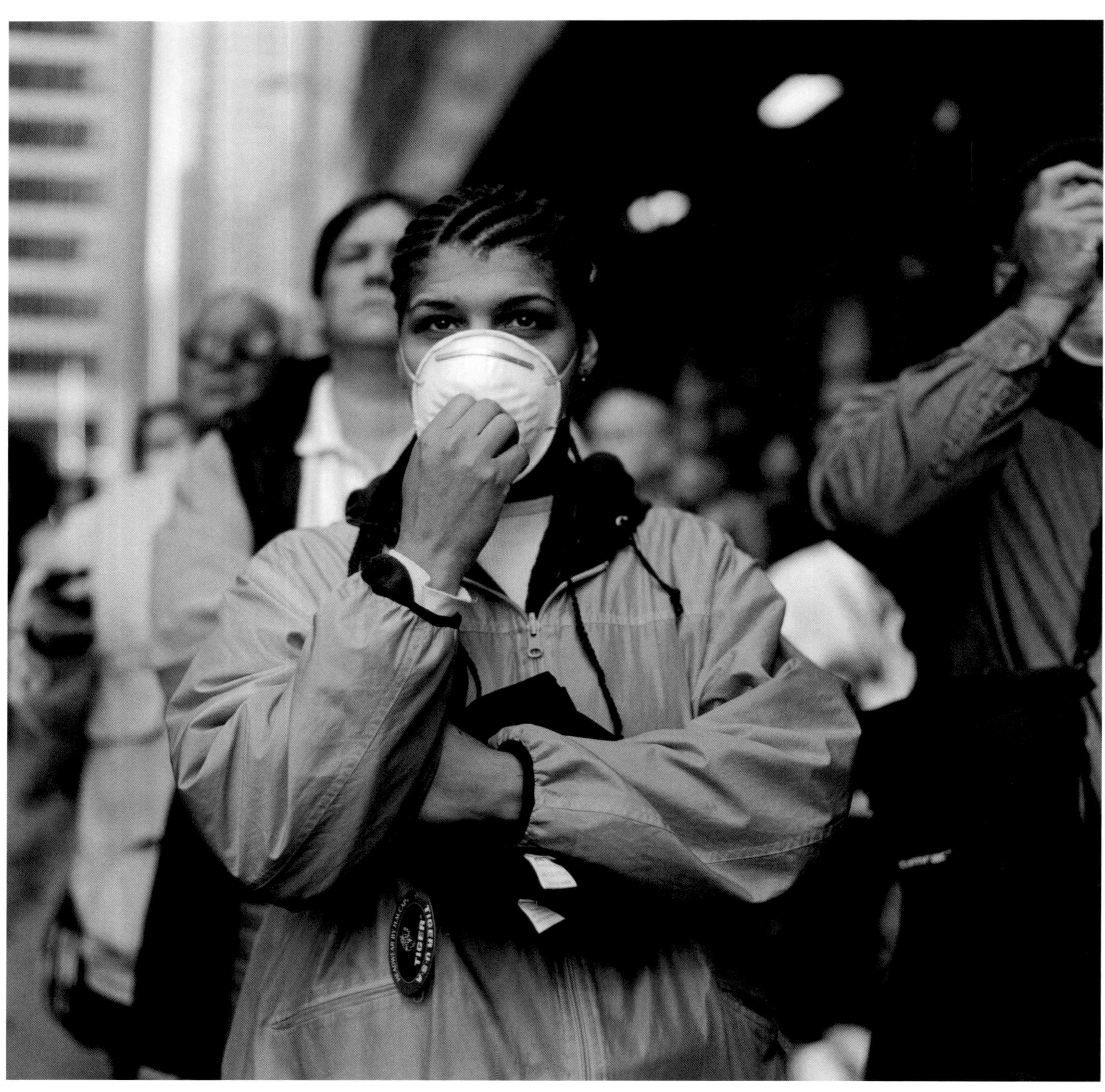
TIGER U.S.A.
TIGER

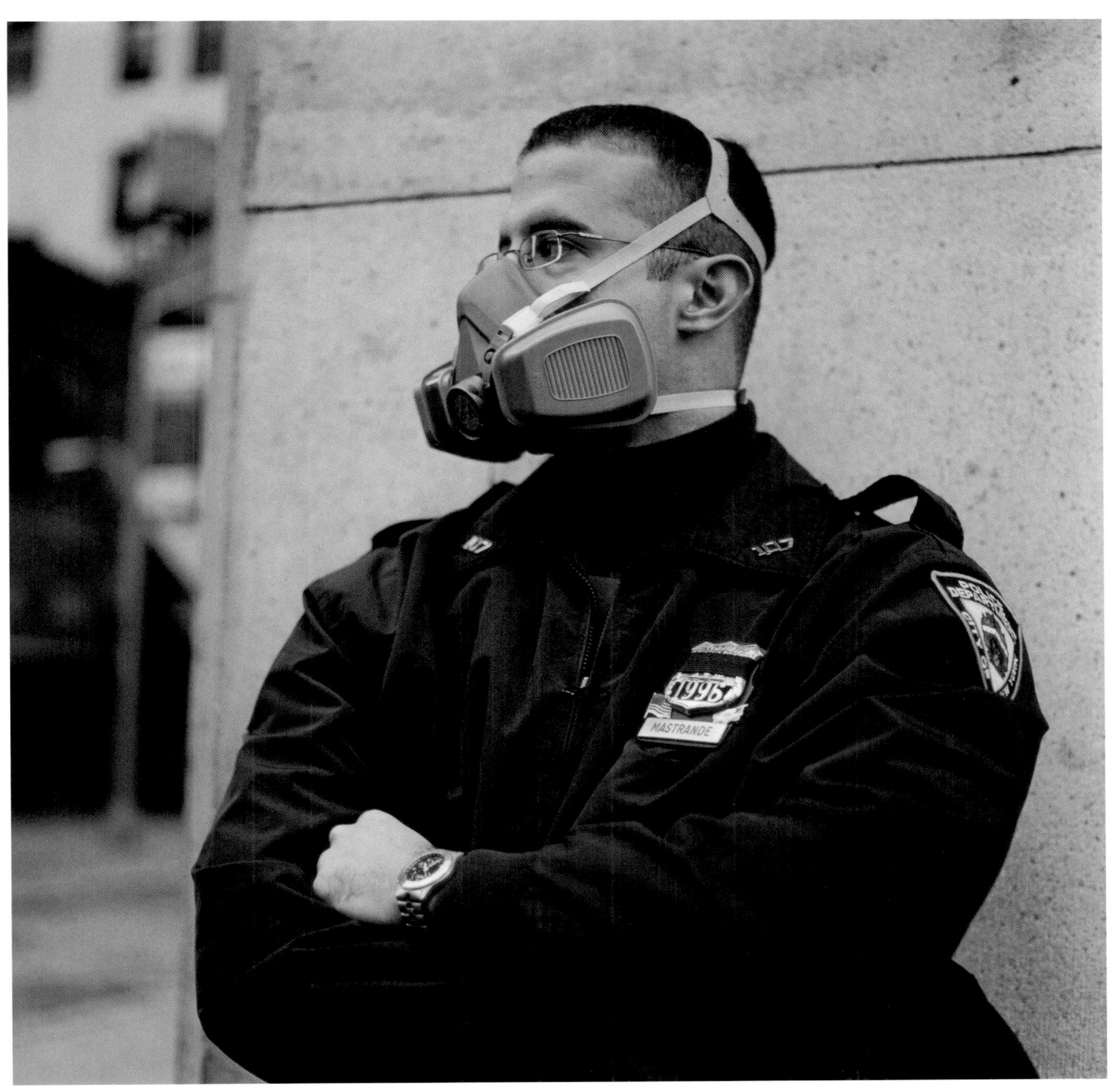
1996
MASTRANDE

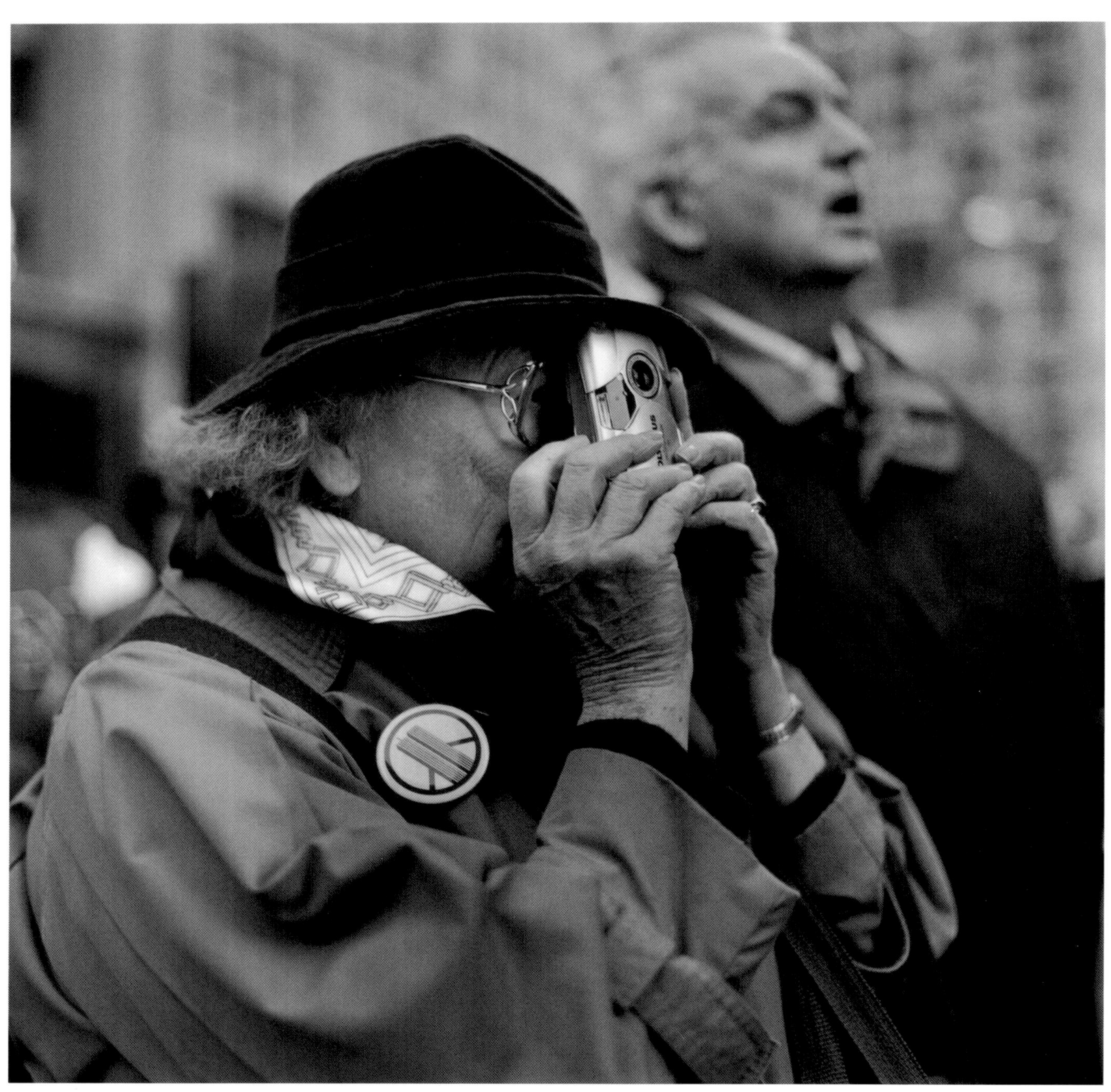

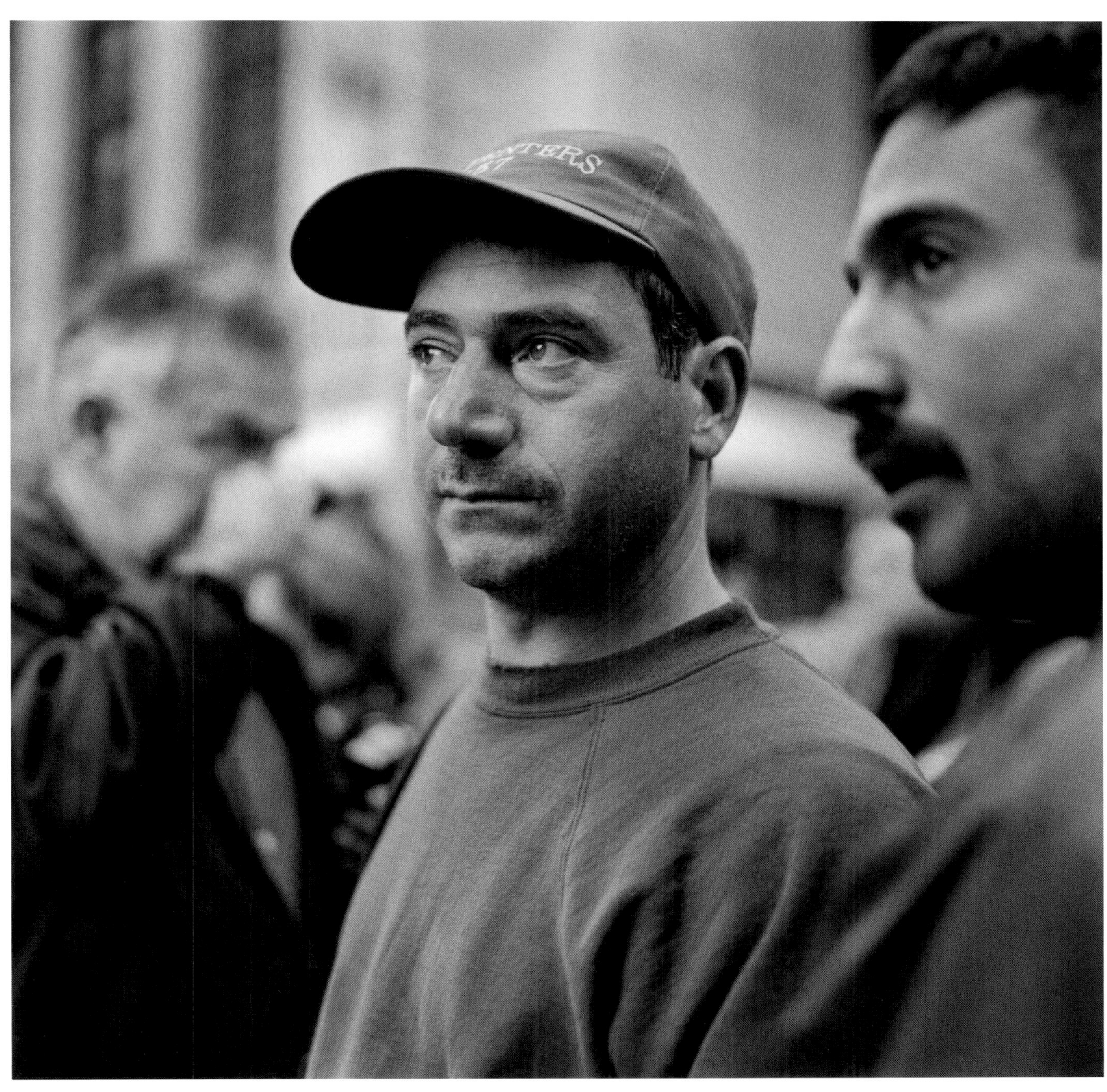

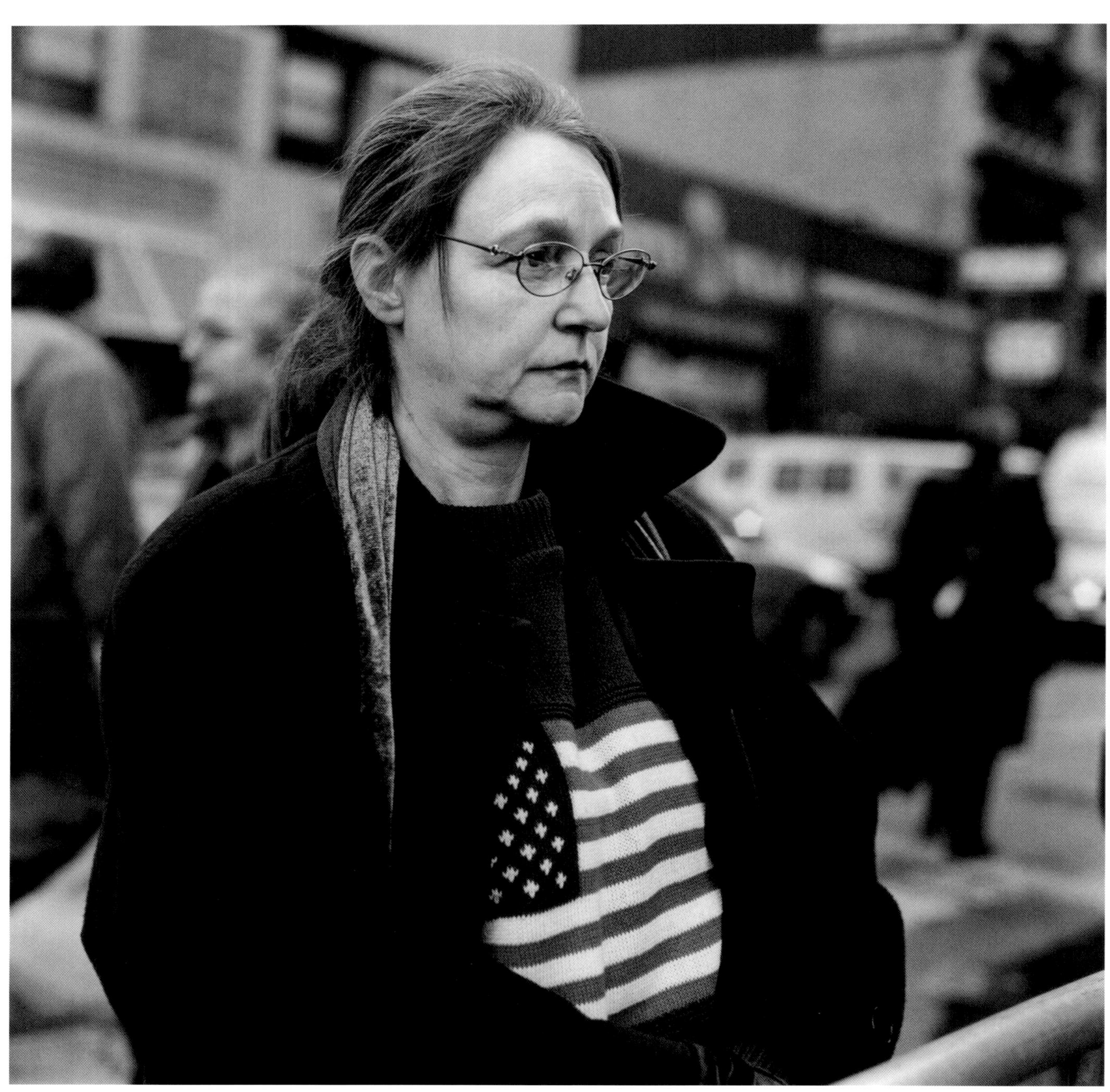

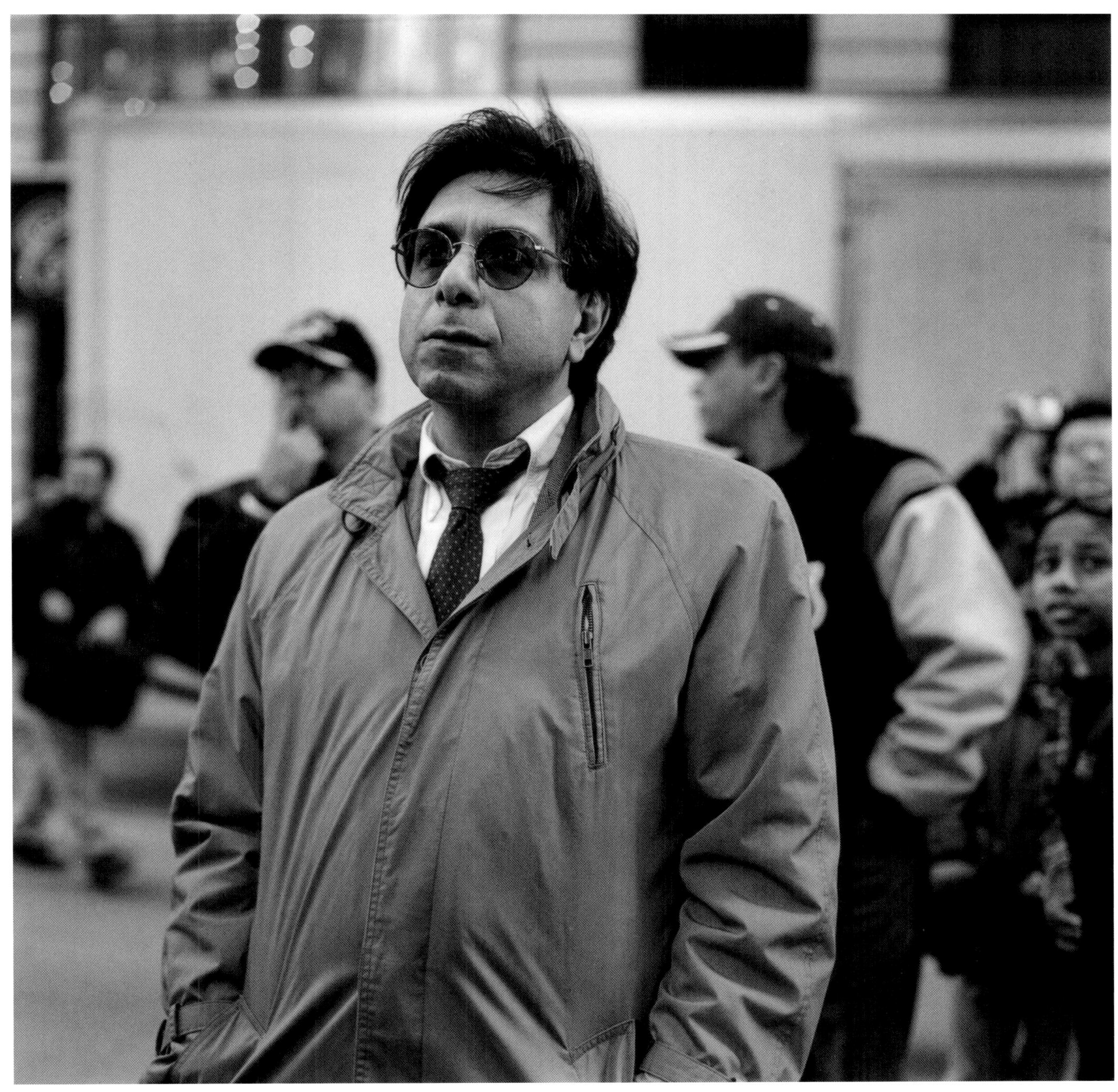

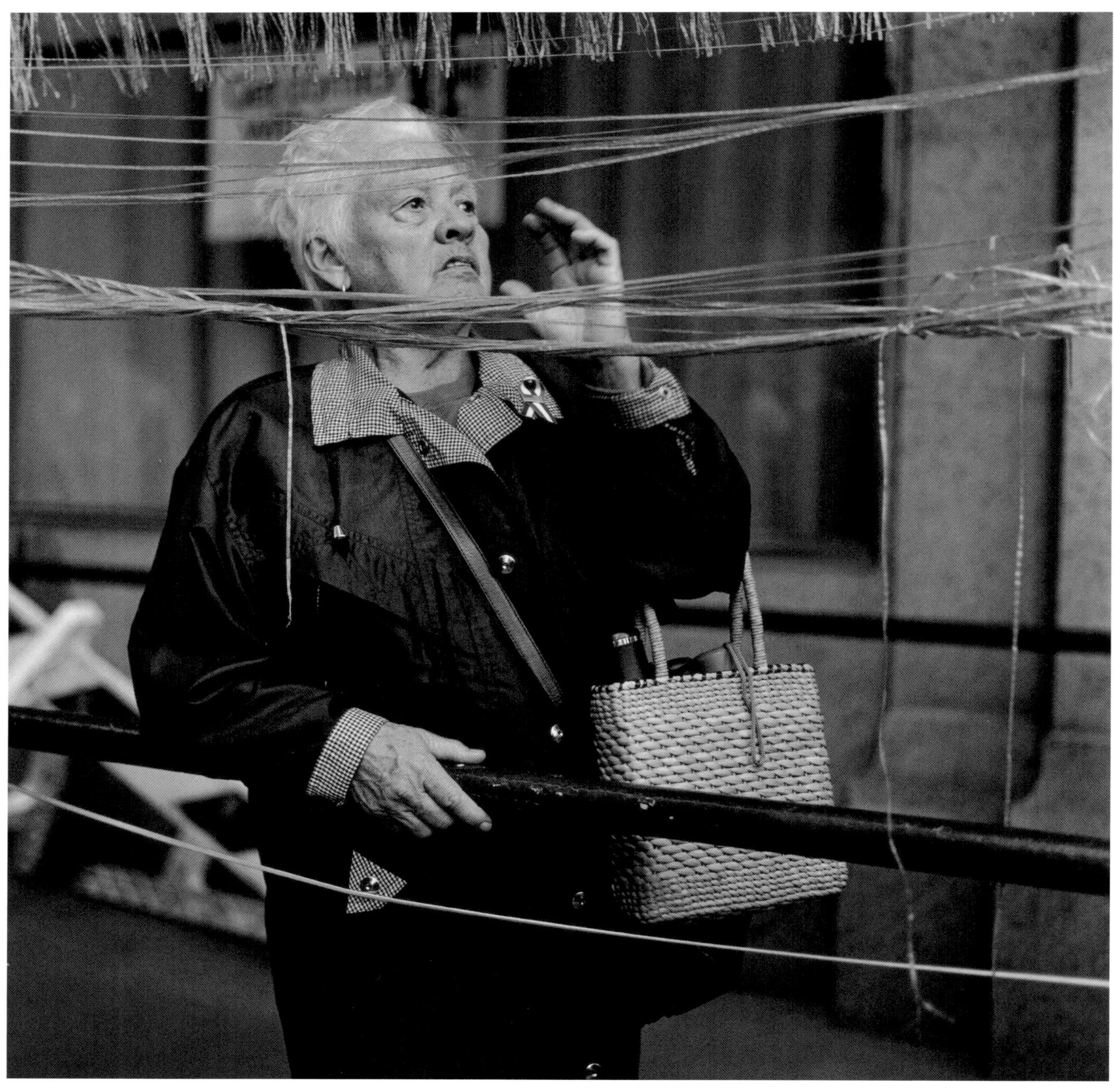

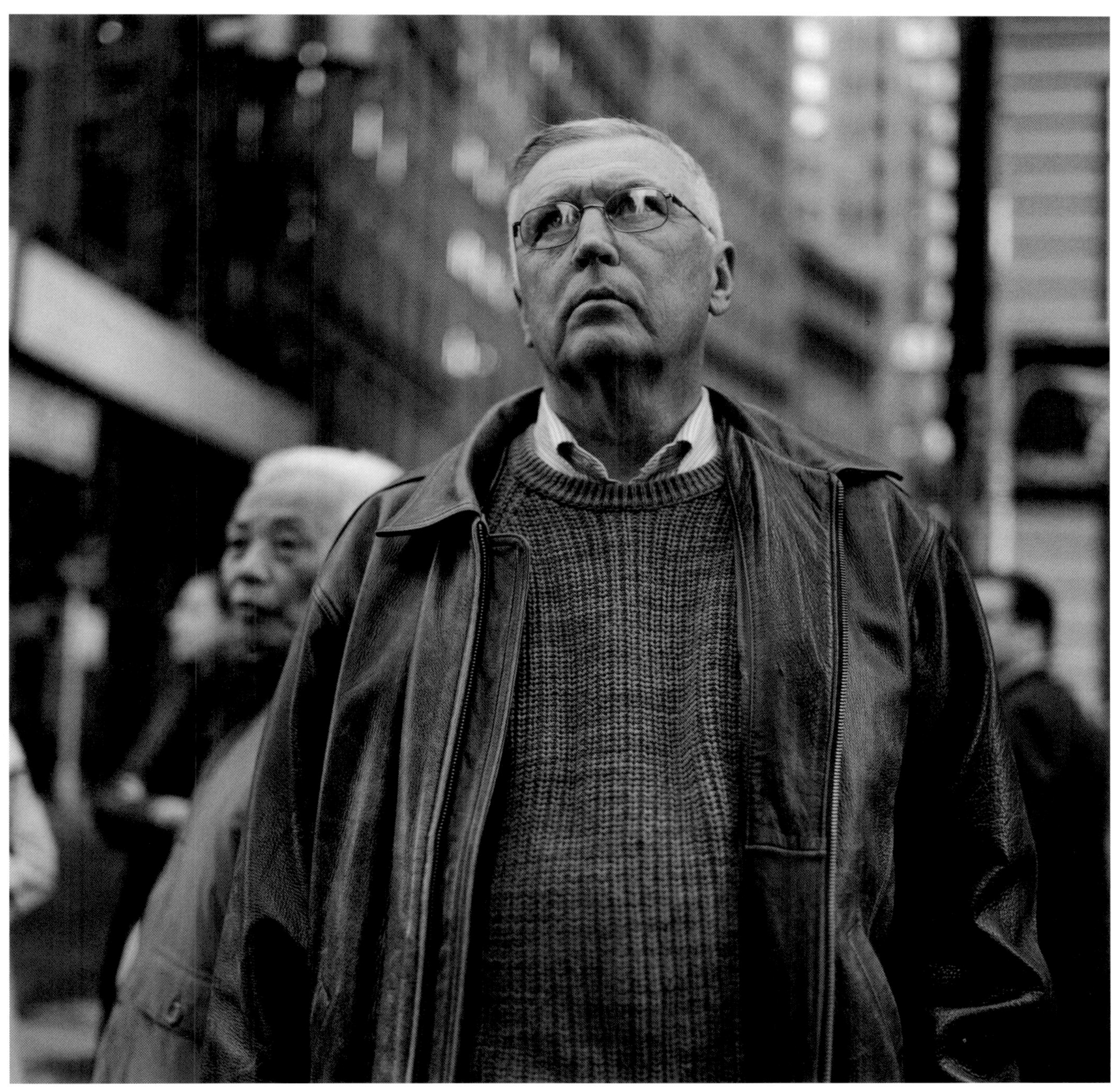

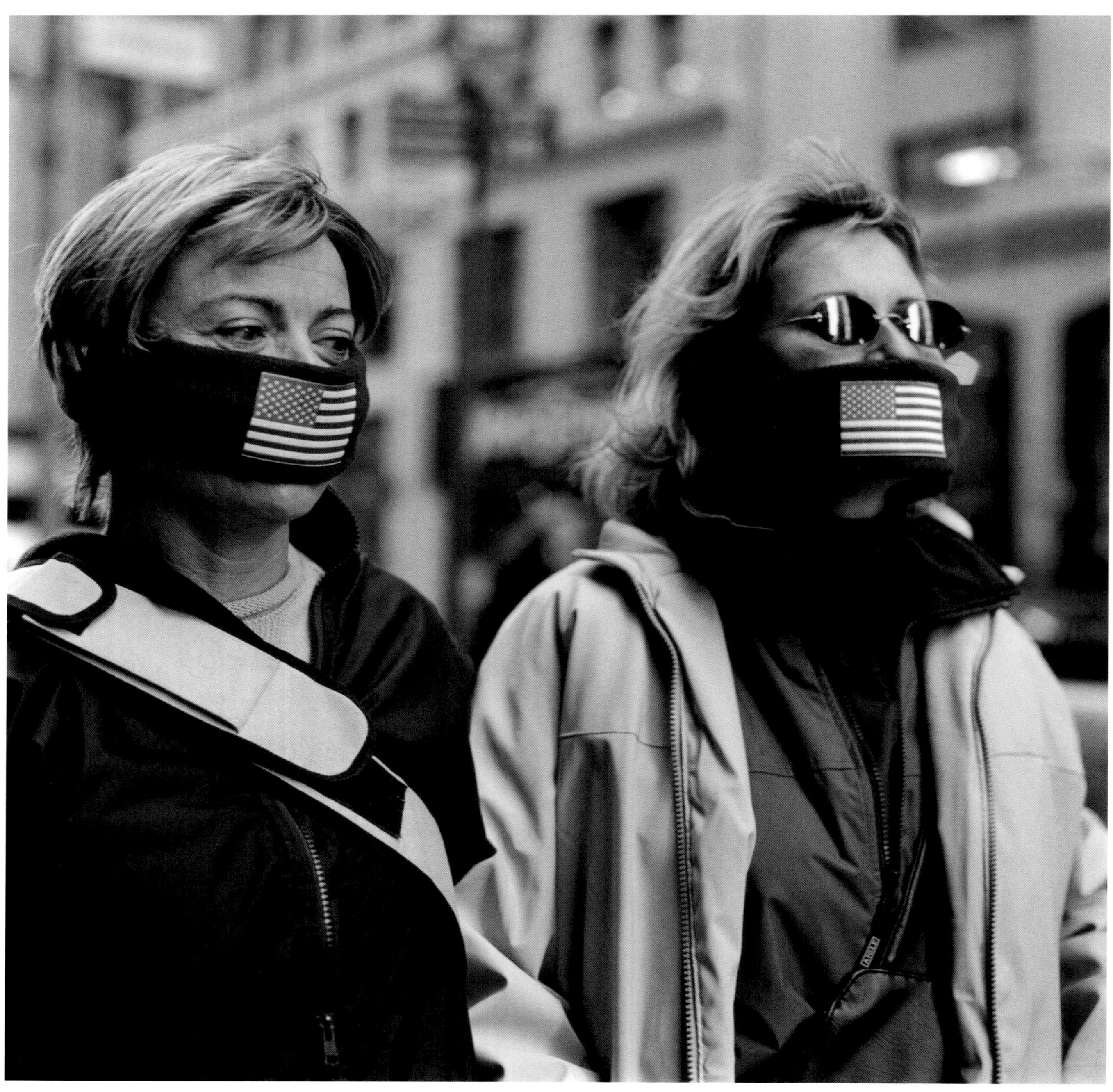

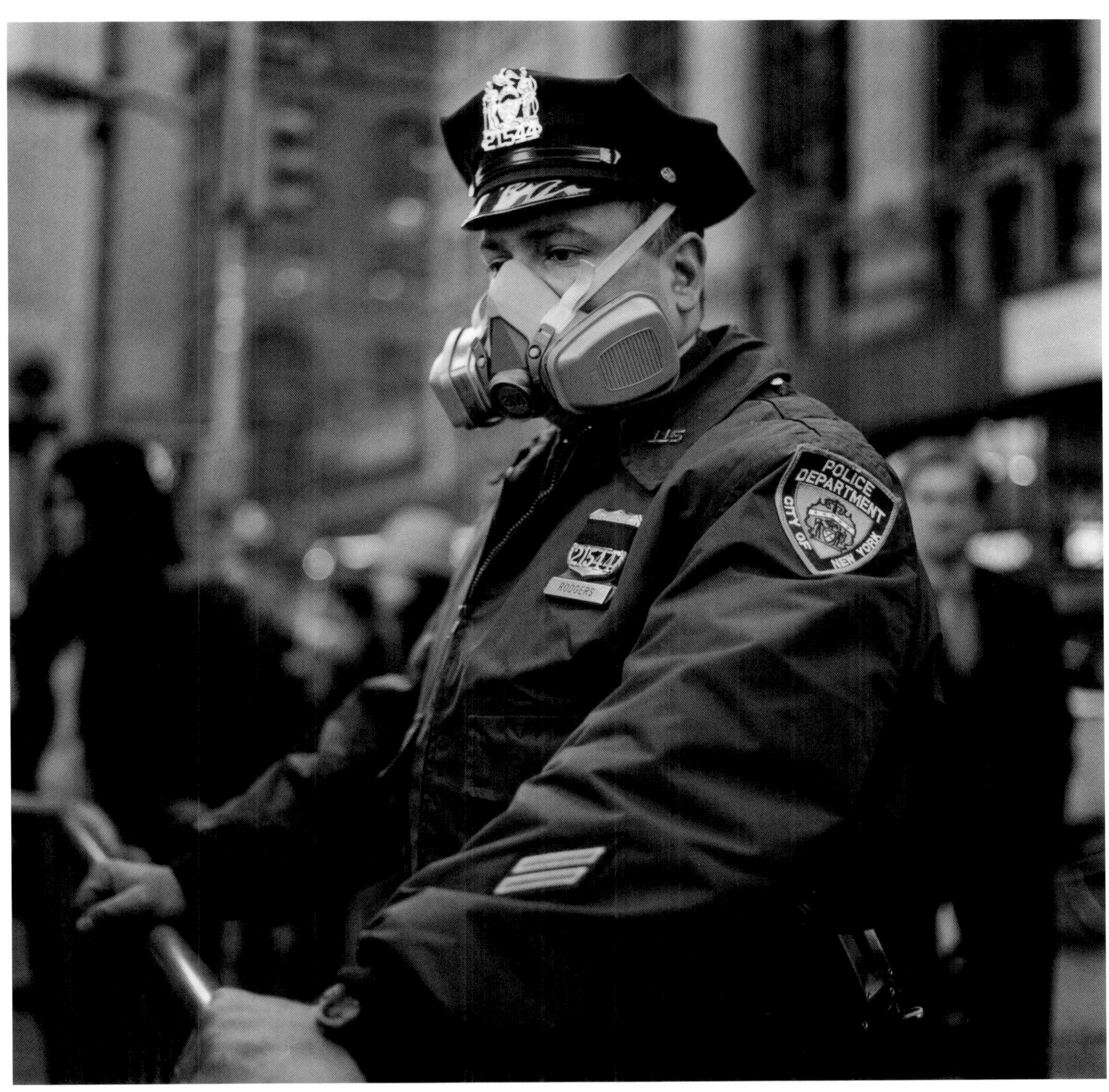
POLICE DEPARTMENT
CITY OF NEW YORK
RODGERS

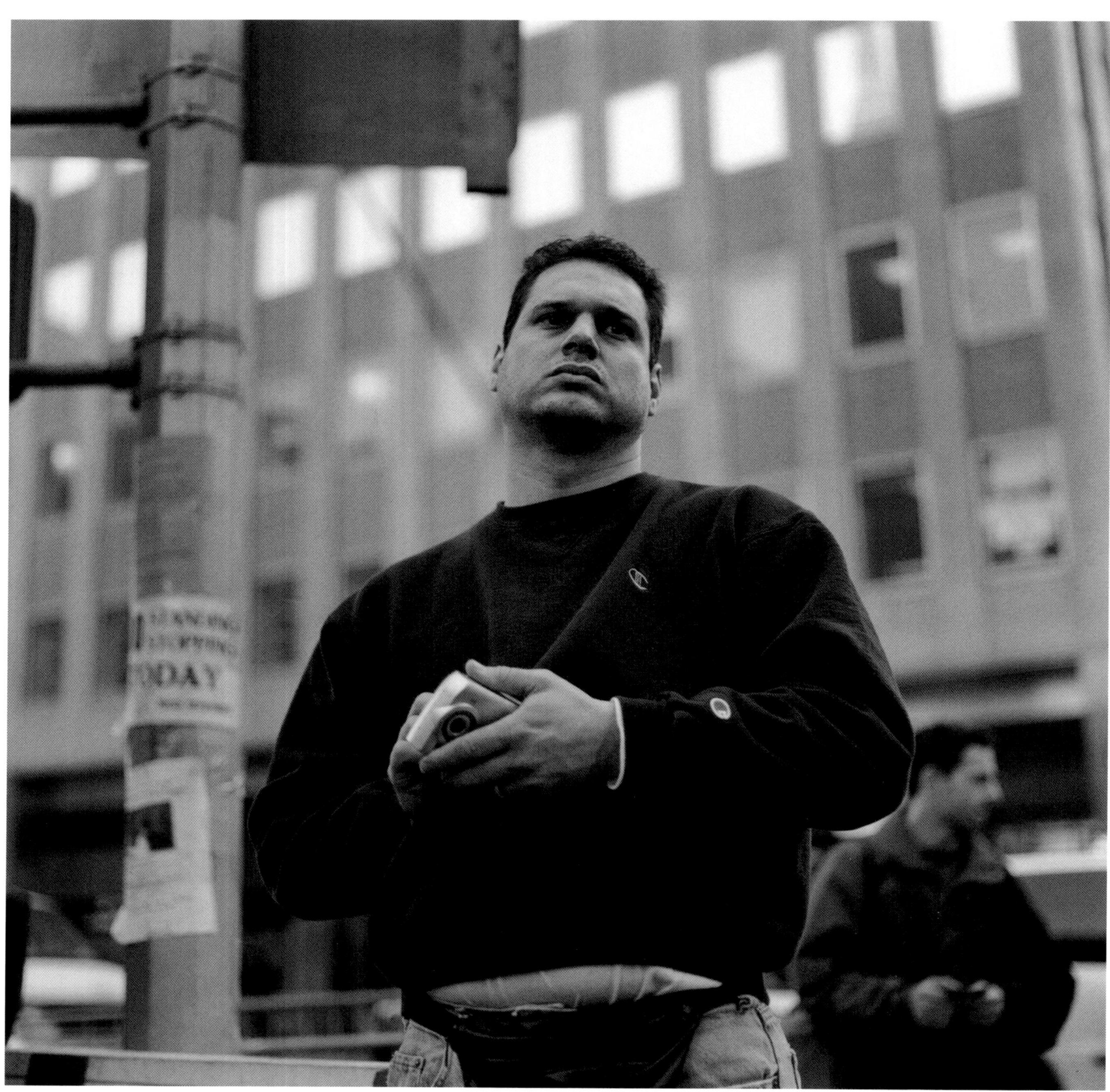

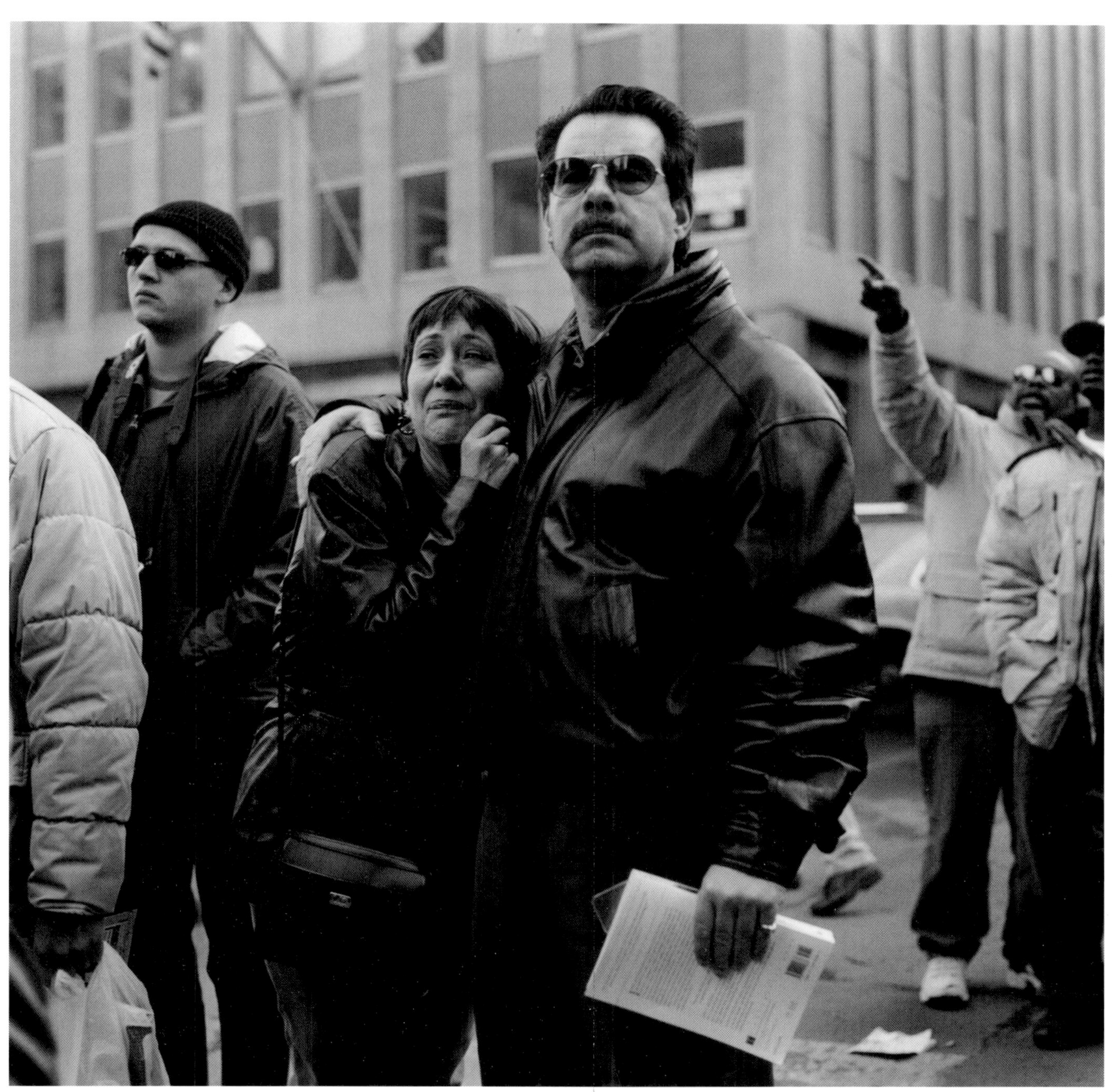

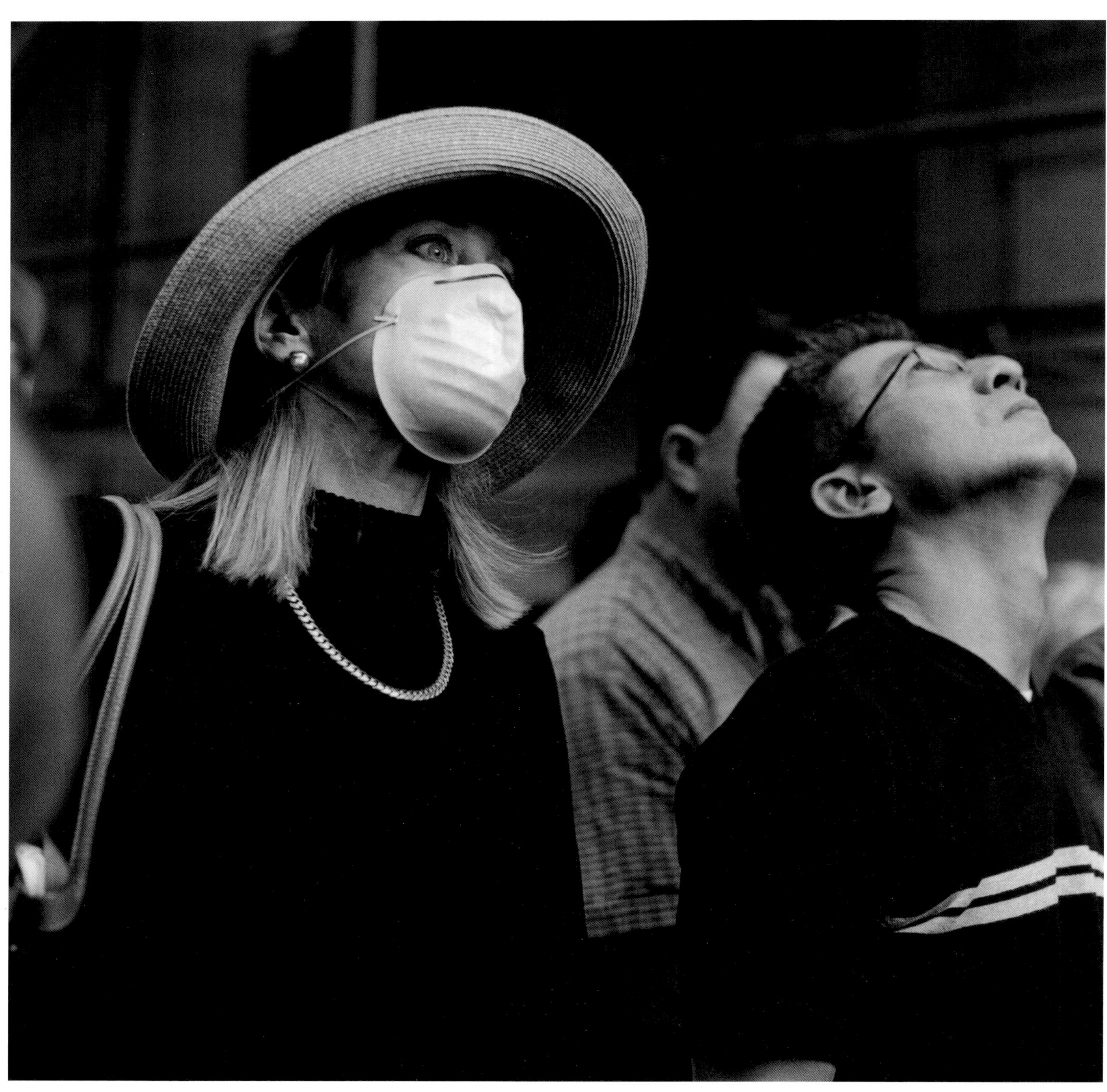

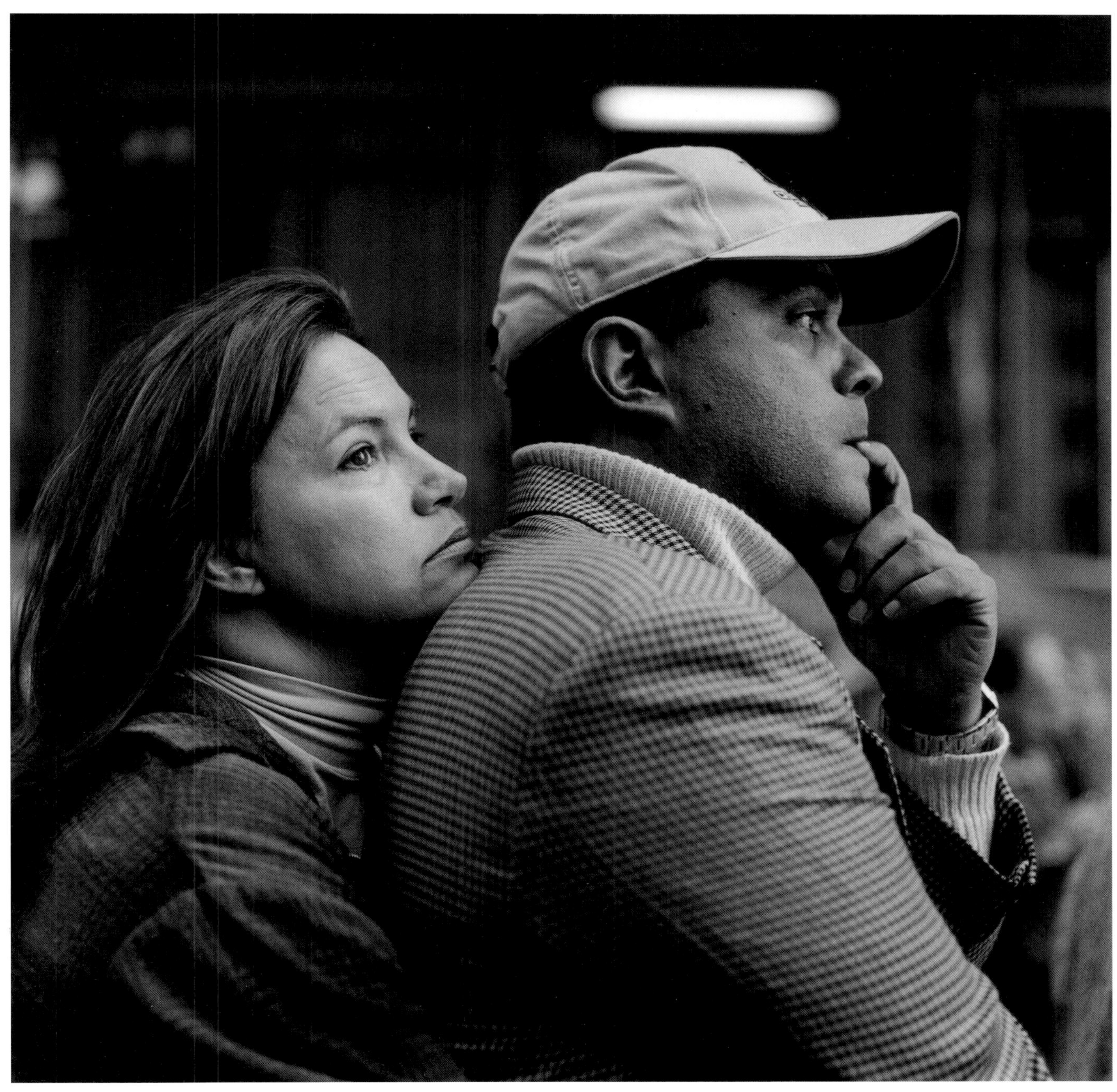

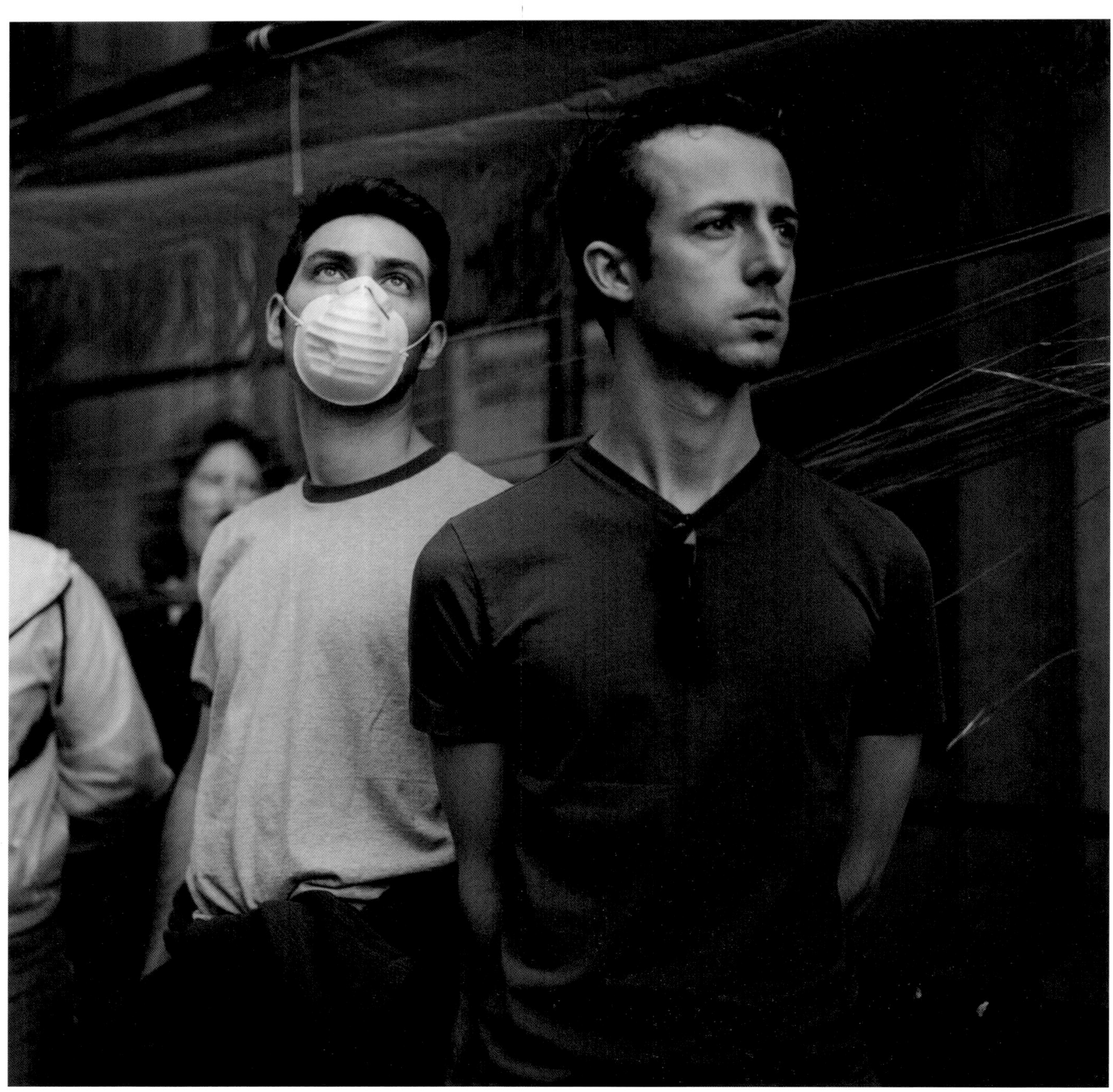

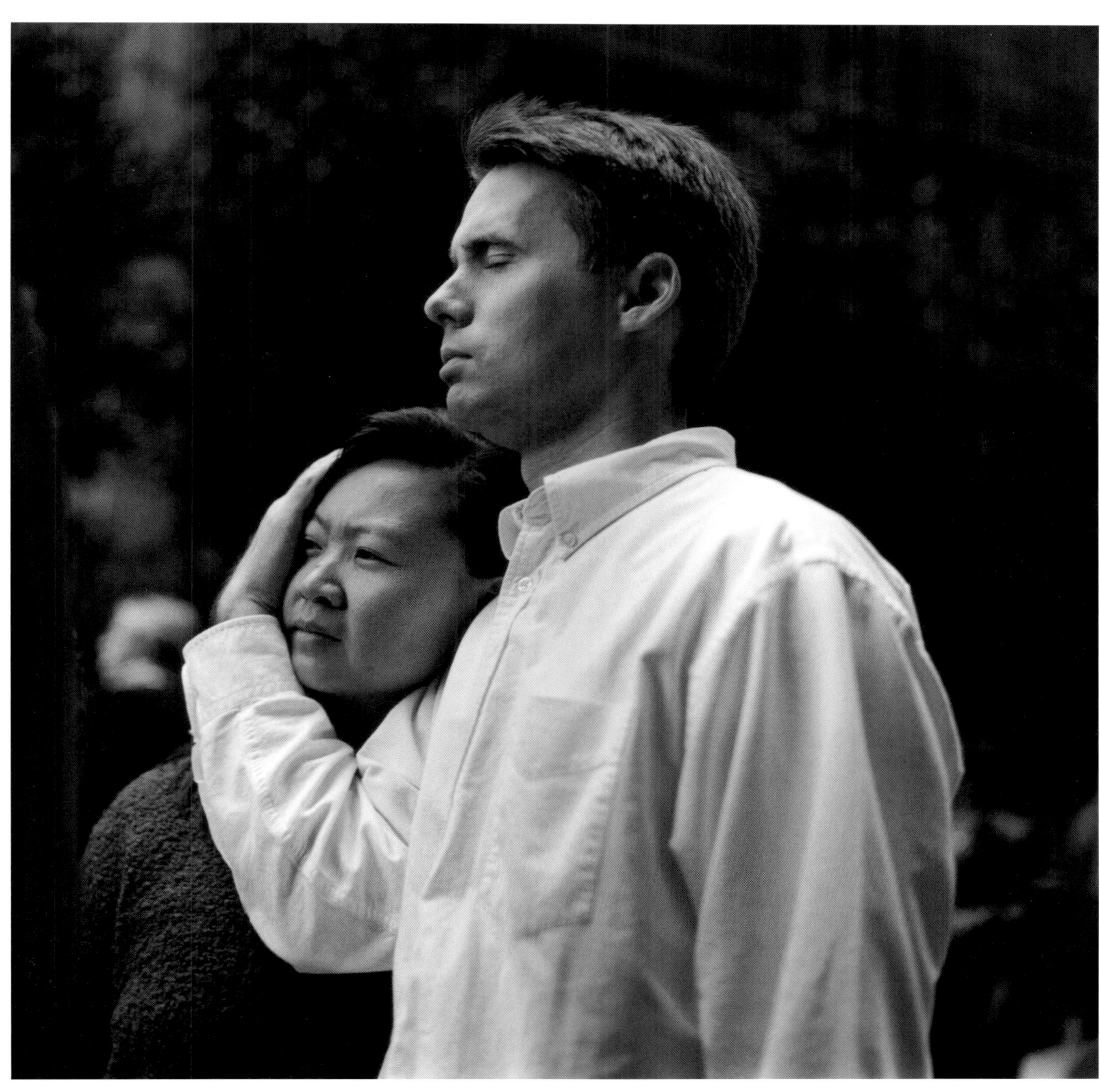

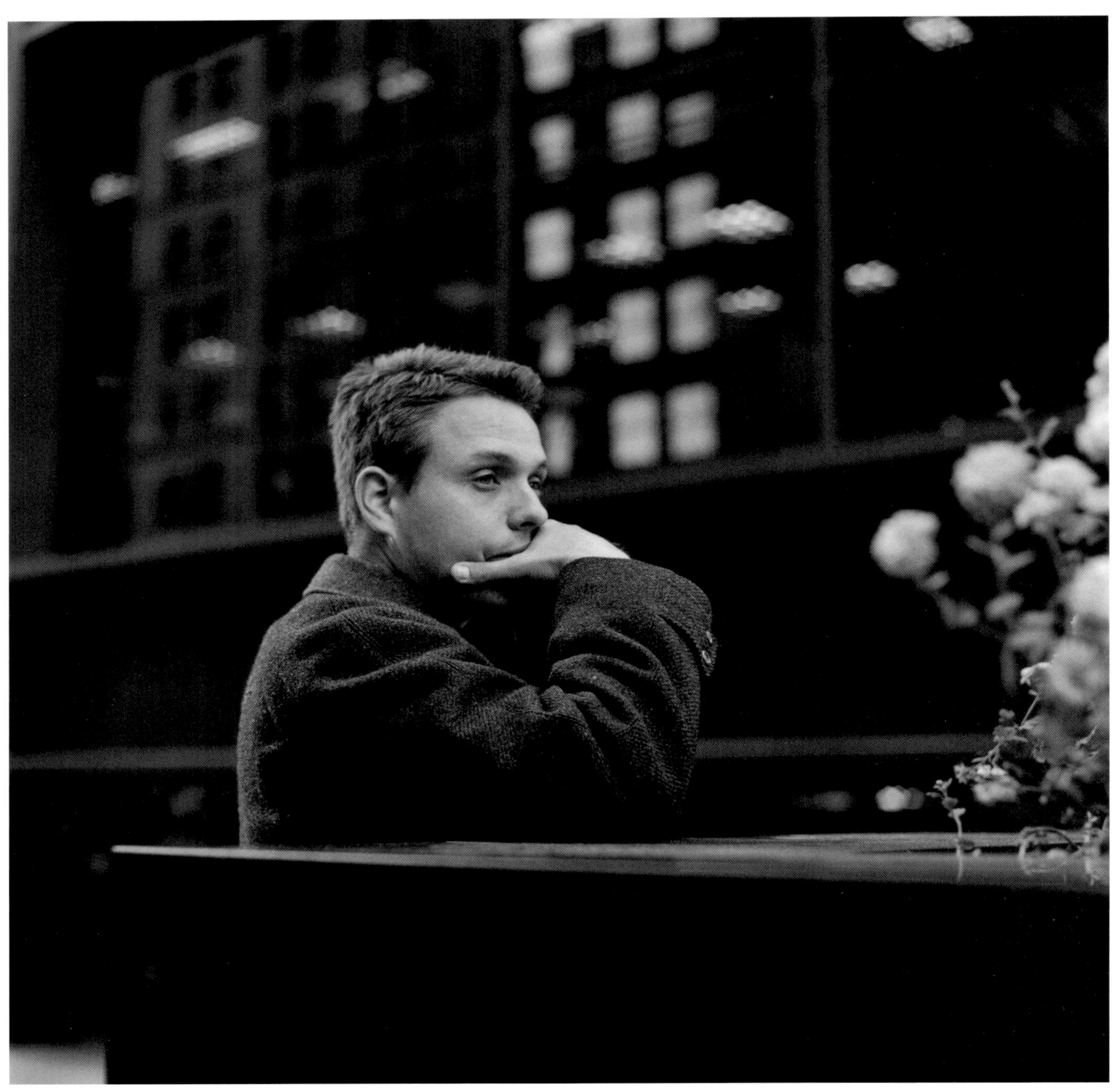

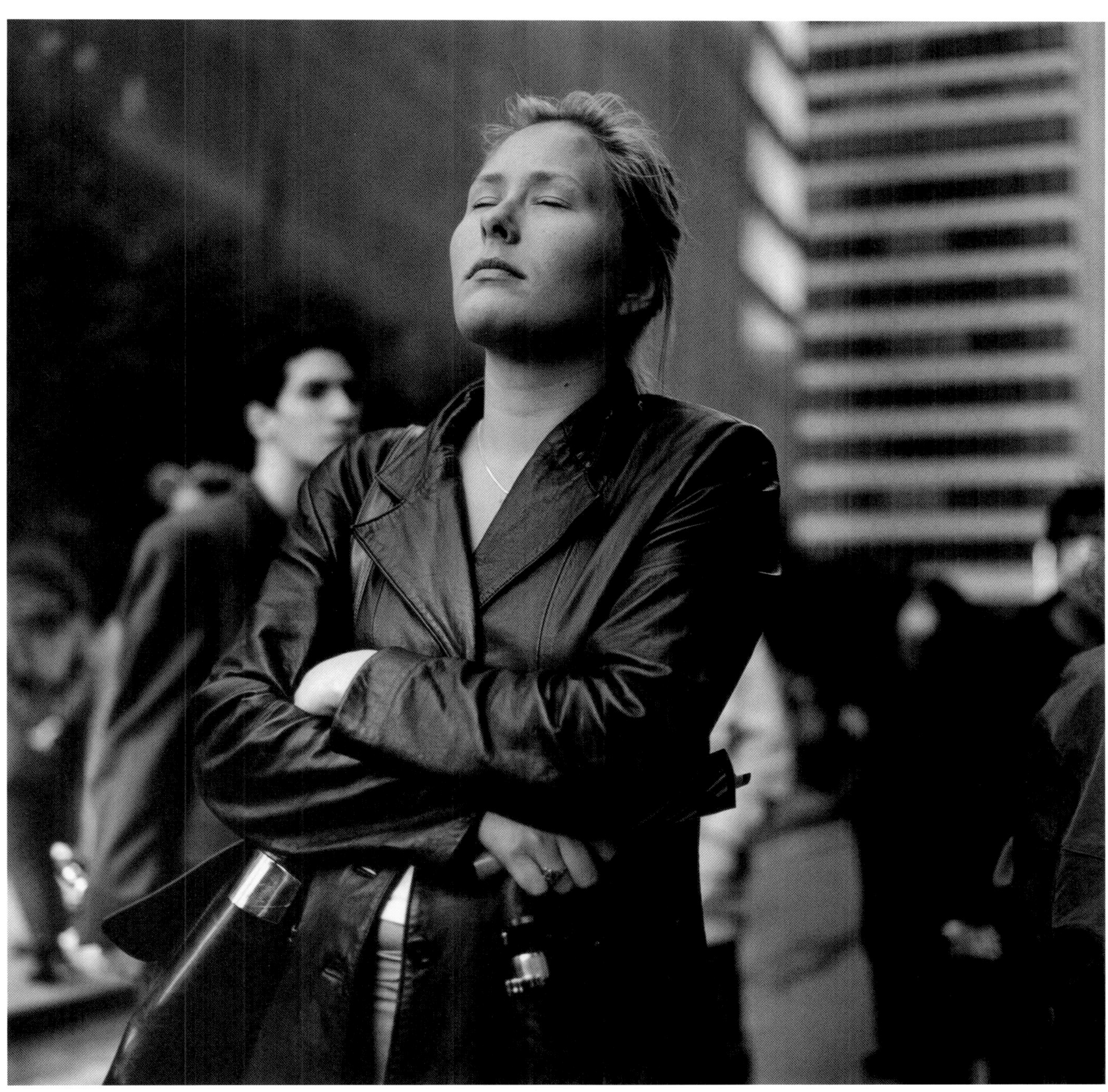

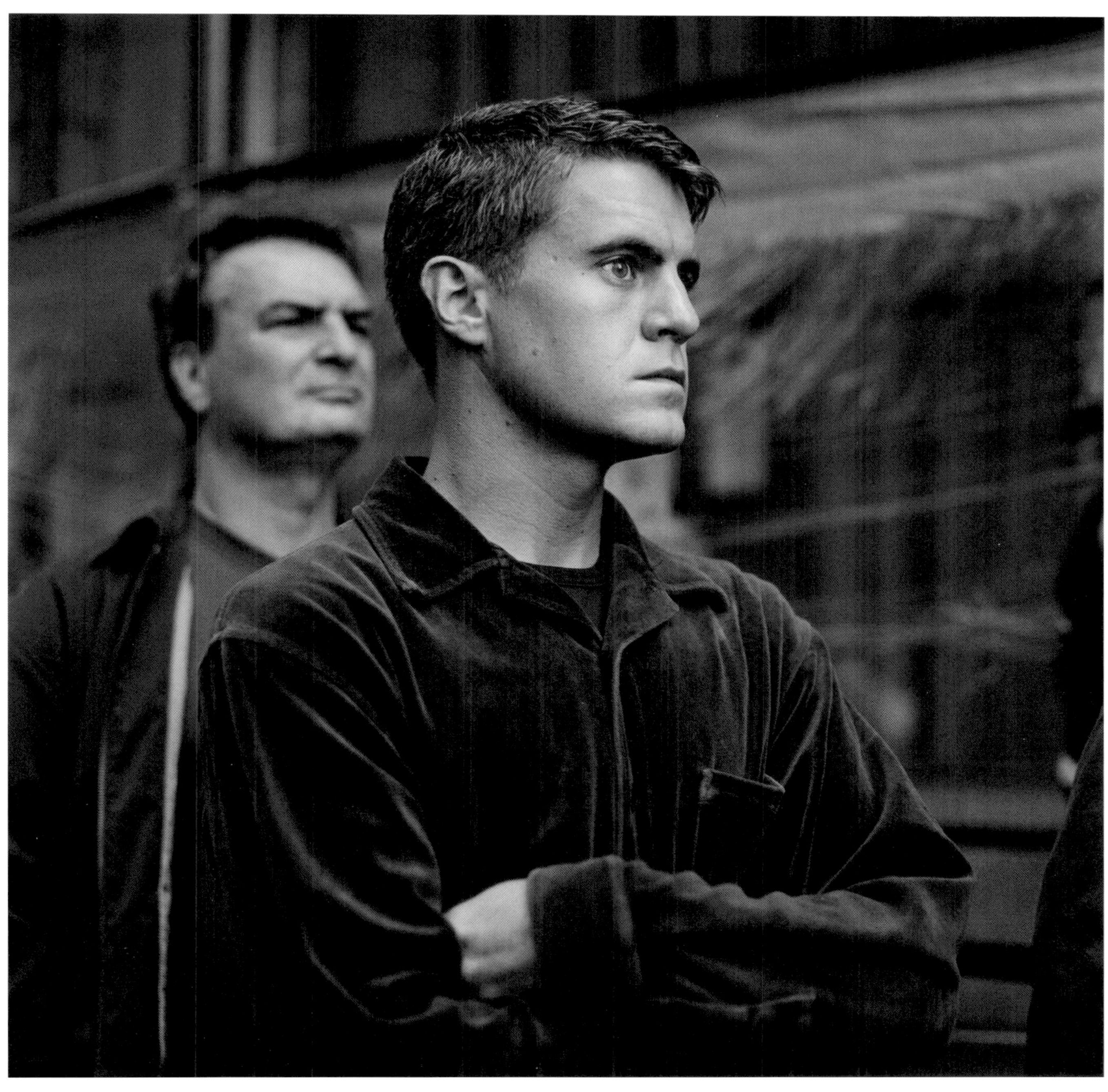

The scale of the World Trade Center was always hard to keep in focus, and never more so than on September 11, 2001. Hidden from plain view by the thicket of other skyscrapers at the tip of Lower Manhattan, the true dimensions of the multi-building site fluctuated or remained obscure from different vantage points. You could be walking only a few blocks away from the twin towers and forget they were there, only to turn a corner and step back, agog. Confronted by them at ground level, it seemed impossible to believe buildings that size could share space on this island with human beings.

An establishing shot that announced "we are now in New York City" to audiences in countless post-1972 movies, the World Trade Center was not, like so many other beloved architectural icons in the city, a single building. As such, it was hard to take to one's heart. The twin colossi rising to an Olympian height of one hundred and ten stories, each floor the area of a football field, were only the most visible symbols of a vast office complex too subterranean and intestinal for complete visual consumption. The mammoth height and girth of the towers seemed designed to cow, even humiliate visitors. Built with public funds, their public lobbies were huge and featureless squares, handling thousands of visitors daily with the charmless efficiency of a sports stadium parking lot.

A sense of the sublime—of beauty and terror—permeates Lower Manhattan. The kicker to the thrill of competing for riches and power in this arena, against the superhuman skyline of Gotham, is the annihilating thought that you don't matter, that the city's relentless energy dwarfs your efforts to organize it; that if you suddenly disappeared, you wouldn't be missed. More than any other city, New York provokes these sensations. The sublime is what attracts people to and scares them about the place; and the World Trade Center offered one of the most sublime views on earth.

It was the science fiction scale of the towers that for many delayed serious understanding of the attacks during the morning of September 11. The first televisioned images, illustrating a report that an airplane had crashed into Tower One at the World Trade Center, showed a blackened crack and wisps of smoke issuing from the upper floors. Cameras had been set up miles away so that the top of the structure could fit the frame. The photographic distance from the buildings, and the medium lenses used, distorted the gravity of the fire. The towers had, in effect, been shrunk to accommodate the format. Only with a telephoto lens, or after some quick multiplication of the data coming through the screen—a small black crack at the top of a building the size of the World Trade Center actually meant a huge three-floors-high-sixty-foot gash—was the impending catastrophe apparent. Then the second plane struck.

The panic that erupted in the mind with the realization that the country was under attack—something that had not happened on the U.S. mainland since the War of 1812—was coupled with television images of flames engulfing the tops of the towers. Their collapse was the most challenging of all to any rational perspective. Constructed side-by-side, girder-by-girder over a period of six years, they came thundering down in less than thirty seconds. Stunned disbelief at the magnitude of this improbability—a shockwave that spread around the world that day and echoed for weeks afterward—has dissipated. But the nausea can return in a flash. If it was hard to believe the towers could exist when they did, it is now even harder to believe that they don't—erased in puffs of smoke along with three thousand human beings.

Kevin Bubriski was two hundred miles away at home in Vermont on September 11. Like the rest of the country, he monitored developments on television and in newspapers. The relentless stream of images and information pumped out by the media in the immediate aftermath was a welcome form of emergency aid. While volunteers dug amidst mountains of rubble at Ground Zero and police attempted to trace the whereabouts of the missing, photographers recorded these struggles and reactions to the crisis around the city. Amateurs and professionals alike felt compelled to take pictures. History was taking shape everywhere you looked.

Two weeks after the disaster, Bubriski and a friend from Japan visited New York. They arrived as the city was recovering from the initial chaos and distress. Hope had faded that any more survivors would be found. Bubriski did not have the special permit required to carry a camera around the site. But seeing people still in a daze, he began to photograph the crowds spontaneously gathering near the corner of Fulton Street and Broadway, a few blocks from the ruins of the World Trade Center.

It is impossible to know why so many decided to make this trip—or pilgrimage, as Bubriski calls it—except to guess that their motives were probably a confusion of the noble and the impure. Photographers are poor mind readers, however closely the lens searches the face. Some of the people in Bubriski's portraits no doubt were already in the area for work; others seem to have detoured from routine and headed downtown out of natural curiosity—to see what could be seen—or perhaps to rubber-neck at the ultimate train wreck. More than a few must have known someone killed or missing. But many likely had no personal connection to the victims or their families.

Bubriski records the motley nature of these crowds to which by definition he, too, belongs, At the same time, his pictures reflect, literally and figuratively, the events of September 11. The violence of that day is treated not by focusing on twisted metal, ripped flags, or debris, but by looking at the faces of anonymous mourners. He is looking at people looking, with somber incredulity, at a monstrous crime. He has wielded his camera in the same way that Perseus did the mirrored shield given him by Athena to slay the Medusa. That Bubriski's indirect glance was also a necessity (by the time he arrived at Ground Zero, the restricted views enforced by police barricades, along with the rapid clean-up efforts, gave visitors little to see) only makes the results more impressive. They are among the most shattering pictures to come out of the event, and the quietest.

Subjects with this emotional scale often require oblique angles to prevent content from overwhelming form. For many other photographers, the side door has been the best way in. One of Roger Fenton's most devastating pictures of war shows clusters of tiny cannonballs among the rutted wastes of the Crimea; it's both the quiet aftermath of battle and senseless litter strewn across a godless landscape. Paul Fusco's heartbreaking book *RFK Funeral Train* dramatized better than any formal obsequies what the death of Robert F. Kennedy meant to Americans. His deceptively simple approach, almost a flip-book, is a series of glimpses at the many sorts of people who assembled beside the railroad tracks to pay tribute to the man as the train carrying his body passed through their cities and towns in 1968. Judith Joy Ross' portraits of visitors to the Vietnam War Memorial in Washington, D.C. explore the limitations of monuments as depositories of emotion. Thomas Roma's recent book *Enduring Justice* is further proof that the best way to tell a story of journalistic import may be to remove all the usual props. His portrait study of defendants and their families, jurors and witnesses awaiting their cases to be called while lingering in the corridors outside Brooklyn Criminal Court points out how closely the complicit resemble the innocent when it comes to photographic profiling.

The spectators in Bubriski's pictures are distinct individuals, but they reflect a collective sorrow. By keeping his focus on the faces and postures of stunned bystanders, he seems to eavesdrop on a series of private moments as well as document a mass demonstration of surging national grief. Everyone in the city during those confusing days will recognize the look and remember the feeling all too well.

The pain is still fresh. Facing west together, they stand alone, in groups, or they hold one another. They are staring into a void and they know it. Photography is the art of the instant. But these views, of people lost in thought and turned searchingly toward the past, seem to last longer than their exposure time. Looking at the absence of something that existed only a few weeks before, they are also aware of staring at a mass grave where thousands of innocents were murdered without warning, as their cups of morning coffee cooled on their desks.

It is too soon to tell if the various analogies to explain the events on and after September 11 will hold. Was the attack on the twin towers another Pearl Harbor? Was it the prelude or the finale to other terrorist acts? Were the men who flew hijacked planes into the towers the vanguard of an army or part of a criminal class, like the Barbary pirates? These photographs won't help answer those questions. The scale of the World Trade Center remains unfixed. But as a measure of what was lost—even if it can't be seen except reflected in the faces of these strangers—these images may lend perspective to the immense shadows the events of that day still throw across the world.

– Richard B. Woodward
New York City
February 2002

Acknowledgments

I wish to express my thanks and gratitude to the people seen here in the photographs.

I want to thank Kudo Taketeru and Rosalie Winard for getting me to New York in late September. My thanks and gratitude to Toby Volkman, Charles Zerner, and daughter Lucia, and to Jeff Janisheski and Miriam Sirota for their hospitality in New York.

My appreciation to Caroline Jackson, Brendan O'Malley, and *DoubleTake* for bringing these photographs to the attention of a larger audience.

My thanks to Daniel Power, Craig Cohen, Jenny Merot Mannerheim, and Sara Rosen at powerHouse Books.

Without the enthusiastic support and encouragement of Richard Woodward, this book would not have happened.

With love and thanks to my wife Laura McKeon and our children Tara and Ryan.

PILGRIMAGE
LOOKING AT GROUND ZERO

Published in the United States by powerHouse Books,
a division of powerHouse Cultural Entertainment, Inc.
180 Varick Street, Suite 1302, New York, NY 10014-4606
telephone 212 604 9074, fax 212 366 5247
e-mail: pilgrimage@powerHouseBooks.com
web site: www.powerHouseBooks.com

First edition, 2002

Library of Congress Cataloging-in-Publication Data:

Bubriski, Kevin.
Pilgrimage : looking at Ground Zero / photographs by Kevin Bubriski ; afterword by Richard B. Woodward.
p. cm.
ISBN 1-57687-146-0
1. September 11 Terrorist Attacks, 2001--Pictorial works. I. Title.

HV6432 .B818 2002
974.7'1044'0222--dc21

2002068434

Hardcover ISBN 1-57687-146-0

Duotone separations, printing, and binding by Artegrafica, Verona

A complete catalog of powerHouse Books and Limited Editions is available upon request;
please call, write, or visit our web site.

10 9 8 7 6 5 4 3 2 1

Printed and bound in Italy

Book design by Jenny Merot Mannerheim

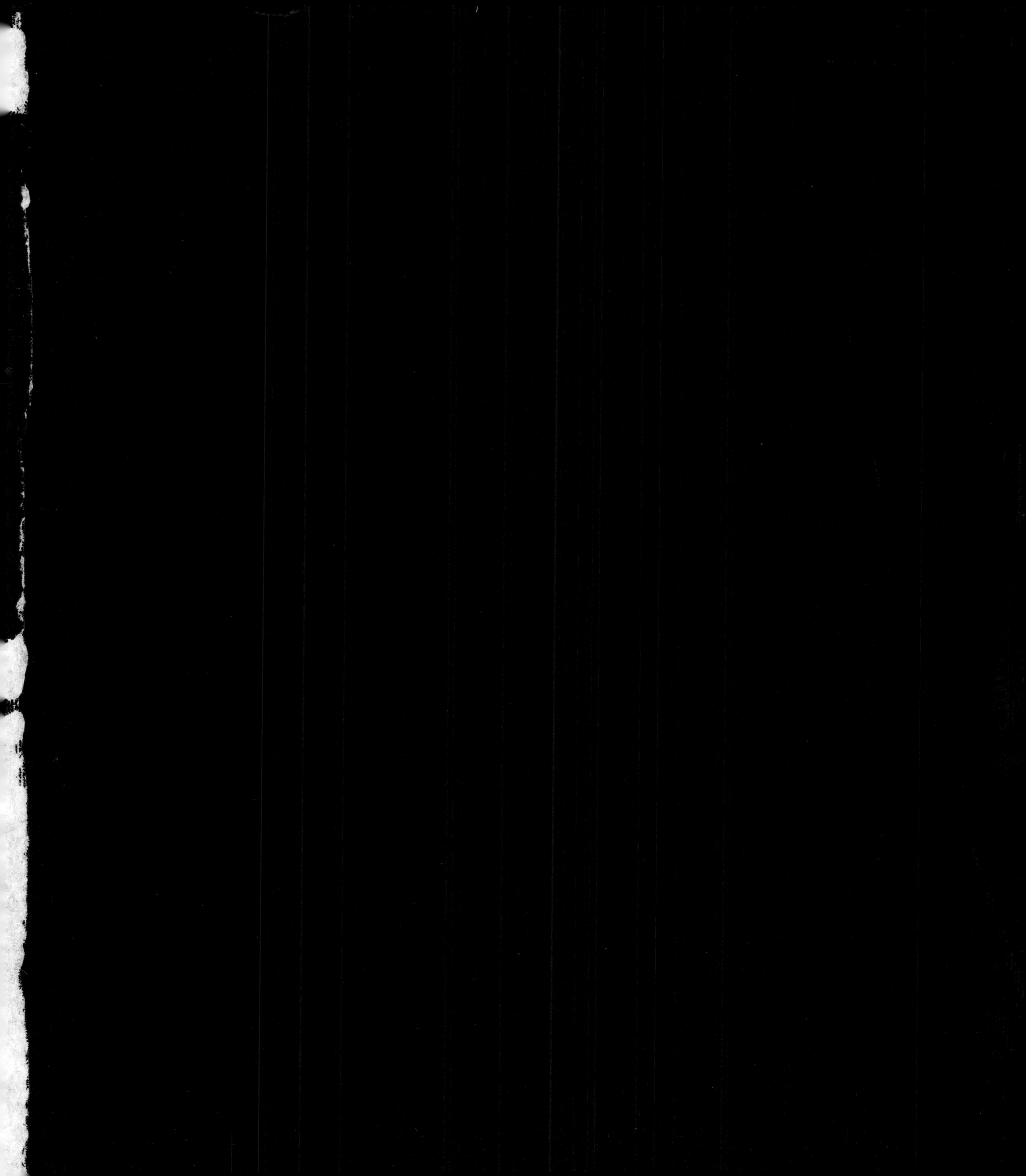